Dream Interpretation: A Biblical Understanding

Dream Interpretation: A Biblical Understanding

Herman H. Riffel

Destiny Image® Publishers, Inc.
P.O. Box 310
Shippensburg, PA 17257-0310

"Speaking to the Purposes of God for This Generation
and for the Generations to Come"

ISBN 1-56043-122-9

For Worldwide Distribution
Printed in the U.S.A.

6 7 8 9 10 / 07 06 05

This book and all other Destiny Image, Revival Press, MercyPlace,
Fresh Bread, Destiny Image Fiction, and Treasure House books
are available at Christian bookstores and distributors worldwide.

For a U.S. bookstore nearest you, call
1-800-722-6774
For more information on foreign distributors, call
717-532-3040
Or reach us on the Internet:
www.destinyimage.com

Dedication

To God, who not only speaks, but shows through dreams and visions what is His perfect and good will for us.

And to many who have attended my lectures and workshops and have expressed being helped by receiving God's guidance through their dreams.

Contents

Chapter 1

The Language
of the Ages

Scientists and Statesmen

We are told that when Albert Einstein was asked where his theory of relativity had originated, he attributed it to a dream he experienced in his youth. According to the story, he was riding in a sled which started going faster and faster until it approached the speed of light, at which time the stars broke into fantastic colors. He said that the rest of his life was a meditation on that dream.[1]

Since we all dream for an hour or more per night, about three years of our entire lifetime is spent dreaming. We now know that uninterrupted dreaming is essential for our physical and psychological health. If a person is continually awakened over a period of time during dream periods, he will become irritated, then nervous, and may even lose his sanity. Whenever a person loses sleep, he must not only make up that sleep, but must also make up the dream time. Alcohol inhibits dreaming; yet some suggest that alcohol makes up dream time with delirium tremens. If God has made us so that we spend so much time dreaming, then surely He has a purpose in it. All through history we find that people have received help through their dreams.

General George Patton received intuitive military guidance from dreams. Robert Louis Stevenson wrote his book *The Strange Case of Dr. Jekyll and Mr. Hyde* from a dream. Dmitri Mendelev developed the periodic table of elements from one of his dreams. Niels Bohr received a Nobel prize for his quantum theory, which he claimed came from a dream. Friedrich Kekule received insight for the structure of benzene from the image of a snake biting its tail in one of his dreams. Elias Howe had a nightmare that gave him an idea by which he invented the sewing machine.[2]

The Scriptures

We need only to turn to the Bible to find a volume of records about dreams and visions. *Strong's Exhaustive Concordance* lists well over two hundred references to such phenomena in the Bible. What is even more significant is that so many great events in the Scripture are hinged on those dreams. Story after story gives evidence of the importance of dreams and visions.

Abraham's call to leave his family and homeland and go to the land that God would give him and where God would make a nation out of him was too much for his mind to comprehend, and what the mind cannot comprehend is hard for the will to obey. So "the God of glory appeared to our father Abraham while he was still in

Mesopotamia, before he lived in Haran" and encouraged him (Acts 7:2).

Once he got to the land, he was afraid, and "after this, the word of the Lord came to Abram in a vision." This vision was probably of a great shield. And the Lord said, "Do not be afraid, Abram. I am your shield, your very great reward" (Gen. 15:2). This must have been a great encouragement to him. Then, as though his mind was still unable to comprehend it all, God put him into a deep sleep in which the momentous covenant was established between Abraham and God.

Joseph was told in a dream that one day his brothers would bow down to him. When he told this to his brothers, just the opposite seemed to happen, the brothers were determined to get rid of their dreaming brother. God, however, was preparing Joseph for greater things. By divine providence, when no one could interpret the Pharaoh's dream, Joseph was brought in to interpret it. Through the dream, God showed Pharaoh the future. But it did not pertain to Egypt's future only; God also had Israel in mind, and the dream gave direction for the saving of His people.

The story of Israel runs parallel to the history of the great nations of the world. It begins with Egypt and in the Old Testament ends with Babylon. God spoke to Nebuchadnezzar through a dream in much the same way He had spoken to Pharoah. The mighty monarch who had built the great city of Babylon and ruled its empire was humbled before God through a dream, which Daniel, a captive Israelite slave, was solely able to interpret.

The greatest event of human history was dependent upon five dreams and three visions; though many people seldom think of it in such terms. Even many churchgoers and pastors are ignorant of the source of this story, though it concerns one of the most familiar events of the Bible: the birth of Jesus, our Lord. It was necessary that the people concerned be told the story by dreams and visions, for the mind and imagination could not comprehend such an unusual event.

The problem of integrating the Jews and the Gentiles into one Church was solved by a vision. The Gentiles were considered heathen dogs by the Jews, but Jesus came to change that concept. Peter, however, the great apostle to the Jews, was not about to let that happen. Peter had been filled with the Holy Spirit and was a deeply spiritual man. Through his preaching he had brought thousands to Christ, and he had even raised the dead. He was an undisputed leader of the Church; yet he could not accept the integration of the Gentiles into the Church.

God knew that Peter's mind was closed on this issue; therefore, while Peter was praying, God played a trick on him. He put Peter into a trance so that his mind would keep quiet. Then, in a vision He showed Peter a vivid picture of the prejudice of his mind, and immediately arranged circumstances that would put Peter into a Gentile home. As Peter stood before the Gentiles, he remembered the vision and suddenly understood its meaning. By means of that vision, God opened the door for the Gentiles to become part of the Church.

For most of us, the very fact that we have received the gospel at all is something we owe to a vision. The apostle Paul had been prevented from preaching the gospel in Asia. He and his companions had tried to enter Bithynia, but the Spirit of God would not allow it. Finally during the night, Paul had a vision in which he saw a man saying, "Come over to Macedonia and help us" (Acts 16:9). The apostle's response to that vision brought the gospel into Europe, and hence to us in the Western Hemisphere.

The New Testament begins with five dreams and three visions and ends with the Book of the Revelation, which is twenty-two chapters of awe-inspiring visions describing the future of the Church.

The Old Testament likewise has crucial events tied to dreams and visions. What would the Old Testament be without the Abrahamic covenant and the formation of the nation of Israel? And without the story of the birth of Christ, Christianity would not know its beginning. Without the Book of Revelation it would not know its end. Dreams and visions were at the center of all these events.

We also have the messages to the prophets, such as in this incident related in the Book of Numbers: Miriam and Aaron were quarreling over their younger brother, Moses. They did not like his wife. In their pique they asked, "Has the Lord spoken only through Moses? Hasn't He also spoken through us?" When the Lord heard this, He commanded Moses, Aaron, and Miriam to come out to the Tent of Meeting. There God said, "Listen to My words: when a prophet of the Lord is among you I reveal myself to him in visions, I speak to him in dreams" (Num. 12:2,6). He went on to say that He spoke to Moses face to face, but to the prophets He spoke in dreams and visions.

We need only read the prophets to see that this is true. Samuel had a vision concerning Eli the priest and was afraid to tell him about it, for it was a pronouncement of judgment (see 1 Sam. 3:15). The writings of the prophet Isaiah begin with these words: "The vision concerning Judah and Jerusalem that Isaiah son of Amoz saw" (Is. 1:1). Isaiah's messages came out of his vision, particularly the one when he saw the Lord on His throne in heaven.

The prophecies of Jeremiah begin with God's question, "What do you see, Jeremiah?" (Jer. 1:11). Ezekiel had some of the most significant, almost fantastic, visions in the Bible. Daniel's writings are a great study of dreams and visions of international importance. Obadiah, Micah, Nahum, Habakkuk, and Zechariah all said that they got their messages through visions. Throughout the Scriptures, dreams and visions are spoken of in a positive way, as a means by which God gives direction, warning, promise, instruction, encouragement, and insight.

Even the dreams of unbelievers are valid. God came to Abimelech, the Canaanite king, in a dream and warned him against taking Sarah. In the dream, Abimelech argued with God and protested that he was innocent of any wrongdoing. He told God that Abraham had said that Sarah was his sister. God accepted Abimelech's protestation and allowed him to challenge Abraham. Laban, who lived in Ur of the Chaldees, had a dream warning him not to do anything to Jacob (see Gen. 31:24).

Egypt was filled with idolatry; yet Pharaoh's dreams originated with God. Gideon was encouraged by the dream of a Midianite enemy soldier and took up the challenge that God gave him (see Judg. 7:13-15). Nebuchadnezzar's kingdom of Babylon had innumerable idols; yet the king's dream was a true picture of his situation and of what was about to happen (see Dan. 2–4). While Pilate was on the judgment seat about to condemn Jesus, his pagan wife sent him a message saying that she had had a frightening dream concerning Jesus and that Pilate should have nothing to do with Him. So we see that God speaks to believers and unbelievers alike through dreams and visions.

That God would continue to speak through dreams and visions all through the New Testament period is stated by the prophet Joel (see Joel 2:28). Peter quoted this prophecy on the day of Pentecost: "In the last days, God says, I will pour out My Spirit on all people. Your sons and daughters will prophesy, your young men will see visions, your old men will dream dreams" (Acts 2:17). There is no hint that God ever intended to stop using these phenomena to speak to His people.

The Church Fathers

We can go to the Church Fathers for further verification of the validity and importance of dreams and visions. Thomas of India received instruction from his dream. Polycarp was given a vision of his martyrdom. Irenaeus had wise understanding of dreams. Clement believed that dreams come from the depth of the soul. Tertullian devoted eight chapters of his writings to dreams. Gregory of Nyssa spoke of the meaning and place of the dream. John Chrysostom called dreams a source of revelation. Synesius wrote great studies of geometry, astronomy, and dreams.[2] Unfortunately, great portions of the Church Fathers' writings about dreams and visions have only recently been translated into English and have therefore been largely ignored.

We know that Constantine was directed in a dream regarding the heavenly sign he was to carry into battle. Therese of Lisieux changed her life through a dream. John Newton, a slave trader, was stopped in his tracks by his dream. In fact, his whole life was turned around and he eventually became chaplain to the king of England. He also wrote the great hymn "Amazing Grace." In a dream, Abraham Lincoln saw his own body lying in state. He often turned to the Bible, where he found descriptions of many dreams.

Dreams and visions are a universal language. We can find rich examples of significant dreams in Israel, Egypt, Babylon, Greece, Rome, China, India, Africa, South America, Australia, and the islands of the seas. No land is exempt from this language, and only the Western Hemisphere has rejected it because of a philosophy we shall explain.

Dr. Ezra Gebremedhen of Denmark was formerly the general secretary of the Lutheran Church of Ethiopia. At the time he told me his dream, he was serving as the research assistant in Patristic Fathers at the Theological Institute in Uppsala University in Denmark.

He told me that while he was writing about the Church Fathers, he became stymied.

"I dreamed," he told me, "that I was stuck in the mud in a marsh and was able to move my leg only with great difficulty. Then a voice came saying, 'Take the shortest way out to dry land'."

The result was that he found the "shortest way" to the materials he already had in this doctrinal thesis, which was all ready. All throughout history God has spoken through dreams and visions. There is no reason to believe He has not ceased doing so today.

Endnotes

1. Jeremy Taylor, *Dream Work* (Mahway, NJ: Paulist Press, 1983), p. 7.

2. Morton Kelsey, *God Dreams and Revelation* (Minneapolis, MN: Augsburg, 1991). (The author speaks at length about the Church Fathers and their interest in dreams).

Chapter 2

The Dangers of Imitations and Neglect

Nowhere in the Bible are we warned to be careful of our dreams. The only warnings are to be careful of the false prophets who have consulted idols or mediums, for they will have false or imitation dreams or visions. God said to Zechariah, "The idols speak deceit, diviners see visions that lie; they tell dreams that are false, they give comfort in vain" (Zech. 10:2).

To Jeremiah, God said, "I have heard what the prophets say who prophesy lies in My name. They say, 'I had a dream! I had a dream!' How long will this continue in the hearts of these lying prophets, who prophesy the delusions of their own minds?" (Jer. 23:25-26). He further said, "The prophets are prophesying lies in My name. I have not sent them or appointed them or spoken to them. They are prophesying to you false visions, divinations, idolatries and the delusions of their own minds" (Jer. 14:14). Later

He calls them "false dreams" (v. 23:32) and "dreams you encourage them to have" (v. 29:8).

God also told Ezekiel of the false prophets who "prophesy out of their own imagination." To such he says, "Woe to the foolish prophets who follow their own spirit and have seen nothing." He says that they have seen "false visions" and "lying visions" to deceive (Ezek. 13:2,3,7,8).

It is of such prophets that God said to Moses, "If a prophet, or one who foretells by dreams, appears among you and announces to you a miraculous sign or wonder, and if the sign or wonder of which he has spoken takes place, and he says, 'Let us follow other gods' (gods you have not known) 'and let us worship them,' you must not listen to the words of that prophet or dreamer. The Lord your God is testing you to find out whether you love Him with all your heart and with all your soul" (Deut. 13:1-3).

As I spoke about dreams to a group of pastors in Singapore, some of them pointed out that their fathers had experienced dreams that told them not to listen to the missionaries. I was puzzled at first, but as we pointed out what God had said about those who go to idols, we soon recognized that this had happened because these older men had come from a corrupted Buddhist tradition; their dreams were influenced by these false sources.

All dreams in the Bible are spoken of as being God's message to be heeded. Other than those warnings about listening to those who seek their communication from evil sources, the Scripture presents dreams and visions as God's instrument. The dreams and visions experienced by those who had given themselves to idols were imitations. Well over two hundred positive references to dreams and visions can be found in the Bible, besides all the examples of the great events that hinged upon dreams and visions and the prophecies that came out of them.

In the light of this evidence, to say that dreams are not a significant part of God's means of communication to mankind is almost ludicrous. Yet much of the Church has accepted a philosophy of the world that does just that.

Plato said that there were three sources of knowledge: the five senses, reason, and the spiritual realm. Aristotle, however, said that valid knowledge comes only from the five senses and reason, denying the validity of the spiritual realm. Many in the western world have accepted that idea, which in turn has influenced the Church. Some in the Church have had difficulty accepting the gifts of the Spirit as valid because they do not come through the five senses or reason. For the same reason, many have denied the validity of visions and dreams, even though the Bible is filled with them.

Many Christians have been duped into believing that the manifestations of the Spirit and dreams and visions are not for today. Some say they were just for the first generation of Christians. Some say they were only for the apostles. If we followed that logic, we would also have to say that the teachings of Jesus and the apostles are not for today.

But nowhere did Jesus or the apostles say that miracles and signs would not be for today. On the contrary, the apostle Paul said, "I will not venture to speak of anything except what Christ has accomplished through me in leading the Gentiles to obey God by what I have said and done—by the power of signs and miracles, through the power of the Spirit" (Rom. 15:18-19). Peter, quoting the prophet Joel, said that God would pour out His Spirit upon *all* people.

Another damaging influence against observing the messages of dreams came through a serious mistranslation of one word by Jerome in the Latin Vulgate. In Deuteronomy 18:10, Leviticus 19:26, and 2 Chronicles 33:6, we are told not to practice witchcraft. Jerome translated the Hebrew word for "witchcraft" as "dreams." From that serious mistranslation the teaching that we are not to observe the message of dreams was carried over into the Roman Catholic Church, which had a great influence on the Church as a whole. Fortunately, the present translations correctly state that we are not to practice witchcraft. It is a serious error to rule out the teaching and examples of the Bible by following a philosophy of the world or a mistranslation of the Scriptures.

Some have interpreted Hebrews 1:1-2 to mean that God ceased to speak through dreams and visions after Jesus came, since it reads: "In the past God spoke to our forefathers through the prophets at many times and in various ways, but in these last days He has spoken to us by His Son... ." However, of this Jesus who ascended into the heavens the apostle Paul said, "It was He who gave some to be apostles, some to be prophets..." (Eph. 4:11). To these apostles and prophets God continued to speak through dreams and visions after the resurrection. Peter was persuaded by a vision to include the Gentiles in the church. Saul, the persecutor of the church, was stopped on the road by a mighty vision. Ananias was told by a vision to go to him, so that Saul could become the great apostle Paul. John then gave us the great series of visions in the Book of the Revelation. So Jesus the Son of God still speaks to His servants through dreams and visions today.

Chapter 3

The Setting of the Dream

All dreams come out of the setting of the dreamer's life, most commonly out of the immediate setting. The picture may seem very strange because of the symbolic language used, but it seems that a dream can give the best possible illustration of our present situation, often in relation to the present time, though it may sometimes be in relation to the past or future.

I once dreamed that I was preparing many, perhaps hundreds, of dressed chickens for shipment.

For a while I could make nothing out of this dream. It seemed utterly ridiculous. The chickens were all nicely wrapped in see-through wrapping and were neatly lined up in great rows ready to be boxed for shipping. But what did that have to do with me? I did not understand the meaning of the dream until I remembered that at that very

13

time I had prepared more than five hundred newsletters to send out to friends. I had sought to put a worthwhile message in them, and everything was ready for mailing. The dream was saying that my letters were like the main course of a chicken dinner that had been prepared for many. This was very encouraging to me and most timely.

Sometimes a dream like that one comes out of the immediate setting of life. At other times it may reflect the past, as when a person dreams of his or her childhood house. Then it probably has to do with childhood experiences relevant to the dreamer's past situation. Often it brings to memory things which have been long forgotten but which need to be remembered and resolved. Sometimes it speaks to a problem on which we are working or a present situation.

While I was in Africa, someone told me of this experience: After much prayer a Zairian man had a vision of the Lord handing him a book that he could not read. The book was then given to the pastor, but he could not read it either. It was a "strong book." He fell down and prayed in another language. He saw the deadness of the churches and continued to pray. As he prayed he saw the Lord standing against the back wall of the church, and he marvelled that the Lord had revealed Himself.

There are times when a dream reaches far beyond the dreamer's conscious experience, as when a friend of mine saw a vivid picture of Native Americans as they lived hundreds of years ago. In awe, the dreamer realized that her dream had to do with her own life, which was too occupied with momentary things. Sometimes a dream will reach far into the future, yet always in some way relate to the dreamer at the time. Sometimes dreams even include the affairs of nations, as Daniel's dreams did, for he was at the time praying for the entire nation of Israel.

We see this principle illustrated throughout the Scriptures. Abram was concerned about the impossibility of Sarah bearing a child when he was given the dream containing the great covenant. Jacob's dream showed the great potential in him in spite of his deceit. Joseph was having trouble with his brothers when God encouraged him through the dream of the sheaves of grain. The butler and the baker in Egypt each had a dream that foretold their immediate future.

The clearest illustration of the setting of the dream is given by Daniel, who said to Nebuchadnezzar, "As you were lying there, O king, your mind turned to things to come, and the revealer of mysteries showed you what is going to happen" (Dan. 2:29). Dreams are often given in just that way. When we have a great concern about a matter, we may well ask God to show us the solution or give us direction, and often it comes through a dream.

Joseph was trying to solve the perplexing problem about Mary's pregnancy when a dream gave him the answer. The wise men were about to tell Herod about the newborn King, whom he would have killed, when a dream warned them not to. Jesus was looking ahead to terrible suffering and crucifixion when He was transfigured. This experience helped to prepare the disciples for His death. Peter's prejudice was the occasion for his vision, for Jesus had told his followers to make disciples of all nations. John was praying for the Church when God gave him the Revelation.

When someone asks me about a friend's dream, I cannot immediately give an interpretation. I need to know something of the setting from which the dream came. It is not safe to generalize, for dreams are very specific. Two dreams from two different people may be very much alike, but may mean something totally different. That was the situation with the butler's and the baker's dreams.

Pharaoh's butler told Joseph his dream: "In my dream I saw a vine in front of me, and on the vine were three branches. As soon as it budded, it blossomed, and its clusters ripened into grapes. Pharaoh's cup was in my hand, and I took the grapes, squeezed them into Pharaoh's cup and put the cup in his hand" (Gen. 40:9b-11). Joseph interpreted the dream, telling him that in three days he would begin serving as Pharaoh's butler again.

The baker saw that Joseph had given a favorable interpretation and, likely thinking that his dream was quite similar, said: "I too had a dream: On my head were three baskets of bread. In the top basket were all kinds of baked goods for Pharaoh, but the birds were eating them out of the basket on my head" (Gen. 40:16b-17). Joseph, however, explained that the dream indicated that in three days the baker's head would be taken from him and that the birds would eat his flesh. Through the dreams were very similar, their messages were the very opposite of each other.

The fact that each dream comes out of the dreamer's setting makes the dream alive and relevant. Therefore, each dream must be examined from the setting of the dreamer's life. This makes dreams a most helpful instrument for counselors. Sometimes a dream will shake us out of our lethargy. I once had the following dream:

I was lying on the sand beside a little stream and enjoying the warmth of the sun and the drifting water. Then

16

suddenly the water began moving more swiftly, and I realized that I was on a flat island of sand and the stream was on either side of me. I could see that soon the rivers would flood the island. My friends were across the stream that I had been lying next to. I did not know if I dared to cross it, and I wakened quite frightened.

To further prepare us for a work we were to be doing together, my wife Lillie's dream was significant:

I was walking carefully under a bridge holding onto the trestle to keep from falling into the river far below. I then traveled on to a flour mill and then to a paper mill.

We later began to realize the meanings. Both dreams referred to my book that was about to be published. The flour for bread and the paper for the book indicated that. The bridge spoke of crossing over into a new territory. The river was the public stream into which we were soon to be caught up. Up until that time I had been comfortably lying beside a little stream of God's blessing, but now I could be swept away if I am not careful.

Chapter 4

The Purpose of the Dream

What great purpose did God have in mind when He created mankind, that we should spend three years out of our lifetime dreaming? Surely it is not for nothing.

Daniel gives us the answer. King Nebuchadnezzar had a frightening dream for which he could find no explanation until Daniel explained to him the purpose of his dream, namely, That you may understand what went through your mind" (Dan. 2:30). A better translation in the Jerusalem Bible says,"That you should understand your inmost thoughts." The King James version says, "That thou mightest know the thoughts of thy heart."

The word "heart" is used here as the innermost organ of our being, from which our motives come. The thoughts of the king's mind were such as this: "I have built the magnificent city of Babylon and rule the Babylonian empire;

there is no kingdom that equals mine. No man is greater than I. I have absolute power over all people in my empire, and can execute whom I will and let live those whom I choose."

The thoughts of his heart were revealed and vividly portrayed in the dream. He was indeed the great ruler of Babylon, symbolized by the head of the magnificent statue he saw in the dream, and other great kingdoms were to follow. However, the dream went on to say that there was a rock cut out of a mountain that was to shatter the statue and blow it away like dust, whereupon another kingdom would come that would cover the earth. These "thoughts" were God's thoughts, put into the king's heart by the dream, over against the thoughts of his mind.

Thus the basic purpose of a dream is to show us the thoughts of our hearts over against the thoughts of our mind. All day long we operate by the thoughts of our mind, with its reasonings and deliberations. When the mind is still, God speaks to our innermost being through the thoughts of our heart in the dream. This balance is essential to a fulfilled life.

The idea of God's will, however, can be manipulated by the mind, as it was when Jacob tried to get God's promise by outwitting his uncle, or when Sarah suggested that Abram have children by Hagar. "The Lord has kept me from having children. Go, sleep with my maidservant; perhaps I can build a family through her" (Gen. 16:2). These were thoughts of the mind.

This is what awakened me to the importance of dreams. I was sincerely trying to be obedient to God's will for my life while serving as a pastor. With my heart I wanted to do God's will, but with my mind I was thinking my own thoughts—until a dream shocked me and set me on my inner journey.

I dreamed that I was enjoying my delightful hobby of mountain climbing. I lived between two mountain ranges in California, and climbing was the kind of experience in which I delighted. It gave me good, hearty physical exercise in a gorgeous setting of high mountain peaks under the blue sky.

In the dream I was on a mountain trail with a high mountain to my right and a deep canyon to my left. The path was wide and my family was following me: my wife, Lillie, a strong resourceful woman; Elaine, nineteen, intelligent and charming; David, fifteen, with a quick head for mathematics and love of detail; Edward, thirteen, blue-eyed and blond, a real nature lover.

The trail was wide ar first, covered with pebbles, but as I proceeded to climb around the mountainside it narrowed more and more. Gradually it became so narrow that suddenly it began to give way under my feet, giving me the horrible feeling that we were all going to slide down into the deep canyon below and would surely be seriously hurt or killed. Having been in such situations in real life, I awakened with great distress and shock.

I had no doubt that God had given me a vivid picture of the thoughts of my heart and the consequences of allowing those thoughts to guide me. With my mind I thought I was doing fine as a father and a pastor, and in actuality it was still so. But through the dream God told me that if I continued to follow the thoughts of my mind there would be a fall that would affect both me and my family. The picture was so graphic that it persuaded me as no mental persuasion might have done to pay attention to the thoughts of my innermost being, and thereupon I paid attention to my dreams.

A dream may show us the thoughts of our heart in many ways. It may come as a warning, as it was in my case and as described by Elihu when he spoke to Job (see Job 33:13-22). Elihu suggested three ways by which God may speak with mankind. He may first speak by word, "Why do you complain to Him that He answers none of man's words? For God does speak—now one way, now another— though man may not perceive it" (vv. 13-14).

If people do not listen to what God tells them, He may show them in order to preserve them from a fall: "In a dream, in a vision of the night, when deep sleep falls on men as they slumber in their beds, He may speak in their ears and terrify them with warnings, to turn man from wrongdoing and keep him from pride, to preserve his soul from the pit, his life from perishing by the sword" (vv. 15-18). He takes this second step to make them aware of their danger.

If, however, they neither listen to God's words nor pay attention to their dreams, there may be a more drastic way that He speaks. "Or a man may be chastened on a bed of pain with constant distress in his bones, so that his very being finds food repulsive and his soul loathes the choicest meal. His flesh wastes away to nothing, and his bones, once hidden, now stick out. His soul draws near to the pit, and his life to the messengers of death" (vv. 19-22).

A dream from the Lord follows the same principles that God laid down concerning divine prophecy (see

Ezekiel 33). If a word of warning about judgment to come is given, it will be fulfilled if the people do not heed the warning and change their ways. If, however, they do hear the message and change their ways, the judgment will not fall. In the same way, if a promise is given to people and they keep their good attitude towards God, the promise will be fulfilled. If, however, their hearts turn to evil, the promise will not be fulfilled.

When young Joseph was promised in a dream that his brothers would bow down to him, the above principle applied. If, however, his heart had hardened against his brothers and he had not forgiven them, though their wrong was great, the promise of the dream would never have been fulfilled. Since Joseph kept his heart right before God even in the midst of great injustice, the promise was fulfilled. He was highly honored in Egypt, and his brothers did indeed bow before him.

A dream has many purposes other than giving warnings. It may give specific direction, as it did to Pharaoh about saving Egypt from famine, and to Joseph, the husband of Mary, telling him when to leave Egypt and where to live. It may give challenge, as it did to Jacob, telling him that the way of access into heaven is always open. A dream may also give encouragement to people in times of great discouragement.

Sometimes God may challenge a person's deepest desires through a dream. Solomon had such a challenge, for he had the problem of trying to "fill his father's shoes," which is a common problem for the son of a famous father. In a dream, God conversed with Solomon and asked him what he would like to have. Solomon asked for wisdom to rule the people, and God was pleased that he asked for wisdom instead of fortune or fame. God gave him the promise of greater wisdom than any before him, plus fortune and fame (see 1 Kings 3).

The Rev. A. J. Gordon, a famous Baptist preacher of Boston, told of a dream that drastically changed his ministry, even though he had never paid attention to dreams before.

It was Saturday night, when wearied from the work of preparing Sunday's sermon, that I fell asleep and the dream came. I was in the pulpit before a full congregation, just ready to begin my sermon, when a stranger entered and passed slowly up the left aisle of the church looking first to the one side and then to the other as though silently asking with his eyes that someone would give him a seat. He had proceeded nearly halfway up the aisle when a gentleman stepped out and offered him a place in his pew, which was quietly accepted.

Excepting the face and features of the stranger, everything in the scene is distinctly remembered—the number of the pew, the Christian man who offered his hospitality, the exact seat which was occupied. Only the countenance of the visitor could never be recalled. That his face wore a peculiarly serious look, as of one who had known some great sorrow, is clearly impressed on my mind. His bearing too was exceeding humble, his dress poor and plain, and from the beginning to the end of the service he gave the most respectful attention to the preacher. Immediately as I began my sermon my attention became riveted on this hearer. If I would avert my eyes from him for a moment they would instinctively return to him, so that he held my attention rather than I held his till the discourse was ended.

To myself I said constantly, "Who can that stranger be?" And then I mentally resolved to find out by going to him and making his acquaintance as soon as the service should be over. But after the benediction had been given the departing congregation filed into the aisles and before I could reach him the visitor had left the house.

The gentleman with whom he had sat remained behind, however, and approaching him with great eagerness I asked: "Can you tell me who that stranger was who sat in your pew this morning?" In the most matter-of-course way he replied: "Why, do you not know that man? It was Jesus of Nazareth."

With a sense of the keenest disappointment I said: "My dear sir, why did you let Him go without introducing me to Him? I was so desirous to speak with Him."

With the same nonchalant air the gentleman replied: "Oh, do not be troubled. He has been here today, and no doubt He will come again."

And now came an indescribable rush of emotion. As when a strong current is suddenly checked, the stream rolls back upon itself and is choked in its own foam, so the intense curiosity which had been going out toward the mysterious hearer now returned upon the preacher: and the Lord Himself "whose I am and whom I serve" had been listening to me today. What was I saying? Was I preaching on some popular theme in order to catch the ear of the public?— Was it "Christ crucified preached in a crucified style" or did the preacher magnify himself while exalting Christ?

So anxious and painful did these questionings become that I was about to ask the brother with whom He had sat if the Lord had said anything concerning the sermon, but a sense of propriety and self-respect at once checked the suggestion. Then immediately other questions began with equal vehemence to crowd into the mind. We speak of a "momentous occasion." This, though in sleep, was recognized as such by the dreamer—a lifetime, almost an eternity of interest crowded into a single solemn moment.

So life-changing are the dreams God gives us. Since we know that dreams are necessary for the physical and psychological welfare of mankind, they must be performing an essential task. They seem to be helping us to keep an important balance in our lives. We know that a dream is doing its own work while we are sleeping. But upon awaking, the dream is pointing up our problem, or solution, or perhaps direction, or challenge or correction.

Endnotes

1. A.J. Gordon, *How Christ Came to Church: The Pastor's Dream* (Old Tappan, NJ: Fleming Revell Co).

Chapter 5

The Importance of Dreams and Visions

Once we realize how important it is that we can actually hear from the God of Heaven, we will then begin to pay greater attention to His nightly messages. God is eager to give us direction, and we should be eager to hear. We might well learn from the attitude that Samuel, the last of the judges and one of the first great prophets of the Bible, took toward dreams and visions.

Samuel lived in a day when "the word of the Lord was rare; there were not many visions" (1 Sam. 3:1). It was much like our own day when, even in many churches, people are quite unfamiliar with hearing the voice of God, and those who have visions are not counted trustworthy.

But Samuel became the last judge and a great prophet of Israel because "the Lord was with Samuel as he grew up, and He let none of his words fall to the ground." Therefore, "all Israel from Dan in the north to Beersheba recognized that Samuel was attested as a prophet of the Lord" (1 Sam. 3:19-29a).

God has much wisdom to impart to His children, both for our personal lives and for the work He has appointed us to do. Some of that wisdom comes when we are asleep, because our eyes cannot see nor our minds comprehend what God is trying to say to us. Therefore, if we fail to heed our dreams, we miss many of the great ideas that God wants to present to us. We may also fail to hear God's warnings in our hour of peril. Dreams and visions are His instruments for that purpose. Unfortunately, many regard their own ideas as more important than God's.

In order to keep from losing what God has for us, there are three important things we must do. First, we must recognize that God is speaking to us today. Second, we must record what He says to us. Third, we must meditate upon what He has said to us. God still speaks to mankind just as He has throughout the past, and He speaks by word, dream, and vision, by day and by night. How He speaks by word I have written about fully in an earlier book.[1] How I came to discover that He speaks by dream and vision is recorded in another book.[2] Now we want to look at the latter more fully.

Most of us have been influenced to think that dreams are rather spurious, insignificant, and not worth much attention. That attitude must be erased from our minds, and it can be if we carefully study what the Scriptures have to say about dreams and visions.

People often tell me that they do not remember their dreams. They no longer say that they do not dream, for unless they use alcohol or drugs, which may inhibit dreaming, these people know that all people dream every night. So why do they not remember their dreams? Most commonly it is because they do not give serious attention to them. When attention is drawn to the fact that dreams are important, a person will usually begin to remember them.

"Daniel had a dream, and visions passed through his mind as he was lying on his bed. He wrote down the substance of his dream" (Dan. 7:1b). We too must make a practice of writing down our dreams. This discipline is not always easy to fulfill; however, if we want to hear what God has to say to us about things that we have not otherwise understood or comprehended, then we will be willing to do that. Dreams have become so important to me that I do not even lie down for a nap without pen and paper close at hand.

There are various instruments available for this purpose. I have found that the simplest is to use a small penlight attached with a rubber band to a pen for recording a dream at night. This way, I do not disturb my wife while she is sleeping. In that way I can pick up the dream quickly and scribble it down for proper recording in my journal the next morning. Often a little one-sentence dream, such as the dream of the dressed chickens in the third chapter, is far more important than we realize.

There are several other reasons for not remembering our dreams. One is a mechanical reason. The radio alarm is perhaps the most damaging obstacle to dream recall. The dream speaks while the mind is still. With the radio alarm, the announcer's voice breaks in upon the mind of the sleeper, and as the person awakens, the dream vanishes away. It is therefore important to allow a bit of quiet time upon awakening so that the dream can have its say. We are told that the best dreams come after seven hours of sleep; therefore, some people never sleep long enough to give opportunity for the dream to speak.

Another reason people do not remember their dreams is because they do not want to hear God speak to them. They are more interested in their own ideas. This was the case with Nebuchadnezzar. Evidently he had not wanted to listen to God in times past, so he had not remembered his dreams until he finally had one he could not forget. If we refuse to pay attention to the dreams through which God wants to guide us, they may turn into shocking nightmares and almost frighten us to death.

Many people need to drastically alter their attitude toward dreams. The proper attitude must not only be established in the mind, but it must be put into practice physically by actually recording the dream in writing. Most dreams vanish upon our awakening and with the intrusion of daily thoughts. We will rarely remember them for long unless we write them down. We therefore need to have a pen and pad, with a light, at hand when we go to bed, enabling us to conveniently record the dream. This can also be done by use of a tape recorder at the bedside. Recording dreams demands discipline, and many of us are not apt to do it unless we are persuaded that this is one of the important ways that God speaks to us, and unless we want to hear what He has to say.

It is important that we record the dream before we start trying to interpret it. If we do start trying to decipher its meaning first, we will be apt to lose most of it before we get it recorded. With the exception of a few cases, most of us lose our dreams within a minute or two after awakening.

Therefore, the dream needs to be recorded, at least by taking notes at night and filling in the details upon awakening. Some dreams may not be understood until years later; therefore, they must be recorded.

It is also important that we all keep a journal of our inner life. In it we can provide the setting of our lives, such as in a diary, and the dreams of the night. We can also record whatever God may say to us in other ways. There are solid biblical patterns for doing this. If David had not recorded his conversations with and about God, we would not have many of his psalms.

Imagine David fleeing for his very life from his own son, and recording his thoughts that night:

O Lord, how many are my foes! How many rise up against me! Many are saying of me, "God will not deliver him." But You are a shield around me, O Lord; You bestow glory on me and lift up my head. To the Lord I cry aloud, and He answers me from His holy hill. I lie down and sleep.... (Ps. 3:1-5a)

What beautiful words we would have lost if David had not recorded the emotions he was feeling when he was hiding in a cave from Saul, who was trying to capture him.

O God, You are my God, earnestly I seek You; my soul thirsts for You, my body longs for You, in a dry and weary land where there is no water. (Ps. 63:1)

Daniel also recorded his dreams. His writings include six chapters of amazing and wonderful dreams and visions, and his experiences with angels that related to them. We would have never been able to read these, as well as the prophecies concerning the return of Israel from captivity, if Daniel had not written them down.

31

The prophets studied the messages they received from the Lord so that they might better understand them (see 1 Pet. 1:10-11). Much of what we read in the Scriptures has come from the recordings made by those who listened to God and wrote it down. We do not know what use God may make of the words that He speaks to us and the dreams and visions He gives us. If we do not record them, however, they will be of little use.

For twenty-eight years now I have kept a journal of my own inner experiences. I began with brief notations, but as my experiences grew, so grew my recordings. For many years, Lillie and I have regularly read good spiritual books and the Scriptures. We then have prayed together about our concerns. After this we sing and worship together. We then sit quietly listening to the inner voice of the Spirit, impressions from God, and write down what we receive. This has proven to be invaluable, and the results become part of my journal, along with my own dreams and their interpretations.

It is amazing how quickly we forget what God has shown us, often within a day or two. By keeping a journal, we are able to refer to what God told us last year. I have recently been reading to Lillie from the portion of my journal recorded twenty years ago. We have been able to check to see whether what we "heard" was really what God was saying, or whether it was partly our own desires. After rereading many of the dreams, we have been impressed with the depth of the messages in them, though at first they were only surface impressions. A dream is often like one scene in movie; therefore it is important to keep a record of your dreams over a period of time. That will provide you with a broader impression of what God is saying.

It is important that you obtain a good notebook or journal for recording your dreams. Each record should include the setting and the interpretation you receive. Though I am reading my private journal to Lillie, I have the option of reading only what pertains to the both of us. Later on, as we look back to the sorrows and inner struggles, we find much valuable material that God has given us. Two of my books came out of much that I had recorded in my journal. I have also derived many devotional studies and sermons. So dreams have become an essential means of direction for me, as they have for many others.

Endnotes

1. Herman Riffel, *Learning to Hear God's Voice* (Old Tappan, NJ: Fleming Revell, 1986).

2. Herman Riffel, *Dreams: Wisdom Within* (Shippensburg, PA: Destiny Image, 1990).

Chapter 6

The Required Response to Dreams

We will not remember our dreams for long if we do not respond to them. That principle applies to the teachings of the Scriptures as well. If we disregard what we hear from God, we will soon lose our understanding of what He is saying. Other interpretations will creep in, and soon we will lose the direction God is offering us.

A woman from New Zealand had the following dream:

I was in my grandmother's garden on a farm in Ireland. Looking at the farmhouse, I saw that it had been beautifully whitewashed and painted and had lovely new lace curtains on the windows. I walked around the side of the house and looked into what I remembered to be the shop window, but now it was a big dining room with lots of tables with white cloths set with lovely silver.

I then walked on to enter into the enclosed farm yard and it too had been all whitewashed and the hay barns were full of hay, overflowing in fact. Some time after having this dream I was praying and the Lord brought the dream before me. I asked the Lord what it meant, and He said, "It's all yours"; again I repeated the question, and again the Lord said, "It's all yours."

God was expecting a response from this woman as He spoke to her in the dream. He had shown her a beautiful scene that she remembered with delight from her childhood. Now God was saying that He was giving her a promise that she should take for herself. Something more beautiful than the childhood scene was being offered, and the challenge was for her to accept it. If she would accept it, it would become hers.

God is gracious and may repeat dreams. He wants us to hear and be guided and protected. Often people will tell me of dreams that have been repeated over some years. When I help them understand the dream and they act on it, the dream stops. We have found that when people begin to respond to a dream, the repeated dream will stop, and God will move on to a new area.

Nebuchadnezzar had not been listening to God; therefore, the first dream that finally got his attention was a nightmare. When Daniel interpreted it and Nebuchadnezzar clearly saw the meaning, he fell before Daniel, acting in response to the dream's message. God pursued him with repeated dreams until he humbled himself and honored Him.

Furthermore, dreams may change as we change. We may have the same kind of dream repeatedly, but as we act on the dream it changes. A person in the dream may be faced by an animal that charges head-on, such as an elephant, a bull, or a rhinoceros. If the dreamer begins to deal with the emotions that these animals represent, then the animals may change. In subsequent dreams the dreamer may see a large cat such as a lion, a tiger, or a leopard, which attacks from behind and pursues the dreamer.

In one case the dreamer said that a huge elephant was chasing him, and he could hardly get away. It was terribly frightening. Then he learned that the elephant represented the great amount of anger within him, expressed by his fierce and uncontrolled temper. He began to learn how his anger could be expressed in a positive fashion, but as yet he had not had an opportunity to do much about it. The symbol in his dreams changed from an elephant to a lion, which was still frightening but at least not so directly. As he continued to learn and act positively, he eventually saw only a mouse, though it was still gnawing on him.

Jacob's dream of the ladder up to heaven with the angels of God ascending and descending on it told him that the way of access to heaven was open for him. Jacob, however, had a deceitful mind and was determined to find his own way. For twenty years he wandered, competing with Laban and trying to make his own way. Finally he was brought to the end of himself and in a vision surrendered to the man of the visionary experience. God waited twenty years for Jacob to respond properly to the dream He had given him.

God likewise often waits patiently for our response. If we fail to respond to the dream, it may be repeated over and over again. If we continue to ignore it, we may not be able to understand the dream, and we may finally be frightened by a terrible nightmare showing how serious our situation has become.

Chapter 7

The Language of Symbolism

The Bible is filled with symbolism. For example:

A great and wondrous sign appeared in heaven: a woman clothed with the sun, with the moon under her feet and a crown of twelve stars on her head. She was pregnant and cried out in pain as she was about to give birth. Then another sign appeared in heaven: an enormous red dragon with seven heads and ten horns and seven crowns on his heads. His tail swept a third of the stars out of the sky and flung them to the earth. (Revelation 12:1-4)

No one would take the above picture literally, for we know it is speaking in symbolic language; yet one of the most common problems with the understanding of dreams is that people do not recognize that dreams also speaks in symbolic language. Therefore, they often fall into the same style as much of the biblical patterns of speech.

Symbolism is used extensively in the Psalms. For example, describing God the psalmist says, "Smoke rose from His nostrils, consuming fire came from His mouth, burning coals blazed out of it...dark clouds were under His feet...He soared on the wings of the wind...He shot His arrows and scattered the enemies" (Ps. 18:8,9,10,14).

The prophets commonly spoke in the same kind of language. Ezekiel proclaims, "The hand of the Lord was upon me, and He brought me out by the Spirit of the Lord and set me in the middle of a valley; it was full of bones...And as I was prophesying, there was a noise, a rattling sound, and the bones came together, bone to bone. I looked, and tendons and flesh appeared on them and skin covered them, but there was no breath in them" (Ezek. 37:1,7b-8). This was a symbolic picture of Israel after its captivity.

Jesus commonly spoke in parables, which is symbolic language. He told wonderful stories out of everyday life which the people could understand. When Jesus spoke of the yeast of the Pharisees, the disciples at first took Him literally, but He explained that He was speaking symbolically. He spoke of Himself as a door, a vine, a shepherd, as bread, and as wine. He did not use the language of reason in describing Himself, for this kind of language is far too limited. Symbolic language is infinite.

While driving through Singapore with a friend, I saw a building with a dome and a symbol on it. I asked the friend if the symbol was a cross. As we drew nearer I saw that it was not a cross, but a crescent. Here we have two symbols, each with a wealth of significance, having very different meanings. Each symbol was identified by one word; yet each would take volumes to describe fully. This demonstrates the depth and the power of the language of symbols.

Symbolic language, though it is deep, is actually the most elementary language. We all learned the language of pictures and symbols before we learned words. Children who are too young to describe their feelings with words can draw symbolic pictures which tell vivid stories of their painful experiences. People say, "Why doesn't God speak in a language that we can understand?" The problem is that we have been trained to be so rational in the western world that we have lost our understanding of the most elementary language there is, the language of symbolism.

Since we have so many foreigners visiting our country who do not understand the English language, we have had to return to that language for our road signs. We now have pictures on our road signs. We also use symbolic language in our political cartoons. A cartoon showing an eagle and a bear fighting with each other proved to be understood around the world whenever I asked people what it meant. They knew that it was not simply a picture of a bird and a mammal fighting, but of two nations being described symbolically.

When we look at such a cartoon we automatically switch from rational to symbolic thinking. That is what we have to do when we seek to interpret a dream. We must think symbolically. With few exceptions, that is the language of dreams and visions.

I often point out that when Pharaoh saw seven fat cows in a dream being devoured by seven thin ones, yet they remained as thin as before, it was not a "weight-watchers" dream! Instead, God was using a natural picture to describe a social condition that was to prevail. While in one area of Australia, I noticed that the cows were fat. This let me know that the crops had been good. In another area where drought had prevailed for several years, I noticed that the cows were very thin.

Dreams often draw their symbols from the dreamer. That is why people often dream of their homes or offices, their work or play. A man dreams of his childhood house. Since the dream reflects the inner life, the house is the emotional, spiritual, or intellectual house in which he lived as a child. Then the dream may show how the trauma of that time period is affecting his present life.

A woman in whose life God had made many positive changes was afraid she would slip back into her old ways of life. She had this dream:

> *I was aware of the sounds of hammering and sawing, construction sounds, and I walked towards these sounds. As I turned a corner, there was the Lord working. I'd never seen my Lord Jesus before, yet I recognized Him! I was stunned that He was doing physical work, and I cried out, "Lord, what are you doing?" Then He turned to me and smiled and said, "I'm fortifying your foundation so that you will never fall." I awoke in tears, at peace within. The fear was gone with His act and His statement of love.*

Sometimes a house we see in a dream is entirely unfamiliar. Usually, however, upon quiet reflection, a memory will come which relates to such a house, and this will be the key to the meaning of the house in the dream. Sometimes the house will be almost like a familiar house, but there will be some differences by which the dream is saying it is reminding you of that association, with whatever differences you noted.

The Language of Symbolism

The meaning of a symbol in a dream does not come by rational thought, but by being quiet, allowing the answer to come from the heart or the subconscious. Neither is the meaning necessarily found by looking it up in some dictionary of symbols, for the symbol comes from the dreamer's own life, and therefore the dreamer alone will ultimately know the true meaning of the symbol.

The woman whose dream I told in Chapter 6 dreamed of a whitewashed house and barn. There are two very different meanings for the term "whitewashed." When I was a boy on the farm, if a farmer did not have money to buy paint, he would whitewash his barn or house, making it look fresh and new. Today "whitewashing" has come to mean covering up, saying, "He has whitewashed his offence." Therefore, the meaning of the symbol "whitewash" will depend on the dreamer's association, and not on the interpreter's idea. I had a significant dream at a time of inner growth in my life:

In a woods, I came across a deserted castle with a moat around it. I crossed the moat and entered the castle, which seemed to belong to me. A big stream filled with logs and roots of trees and debris flowed in front of the castle. The water was swift and came boiling through all the debris.

Then I saw a big Canada goose in the water upstream from all the logs. The goose floated down the stream and then went under the logs, coming up on the other side. As it came up, its head and long neck came through a hole in a log, but it could not pull its body through. Becoming tired, the goose fell back into the water, and I did not see it come up again.

The woods seem to speak of concentrated growth, and my training was indeed intense at that time. A castle is the grandest form of a house. But that castle was still deserted, for up to that time I had not advanced far enough to live in a spiritual castle. The moat around the castle spoke of the castle's protection. It could not be entered except by the draw bridge that could be let down. I realized that I could not enter the castle of my soul without walking across the proper bridge.

I began to cross that bridge and enter the castle as I prayed for further growth. However, there was a spiritual part of me that was stuck with its head in the hole in the log. A goose can fly, walk, and dive. Likewise, the soul can fly into spiritual heights, walk slowly and faithfully, or dive into the depths of the heart, the subconscious, after the "treasures of darkness, riches stored in secret places" (Is. 45:3).

The log was the tree that was holding me down, for the church I was in did not allow for further spiritual growth and expression. The tree has annual rings, "line upon line" of teaching. I had to escape from that and fly, which took place by the release of the Spirit in my life. The goose also migrates, as I have done since.

Thy symbols of a dream are infinite, just as our experiences are. The car is a cultural symbol. In many of our western countries it is the most available means for getting around. It may speak of our ego self. The person driving the car is in control. But it may be like the dream of a seventeen-year-old girl I know. She told me:

I was driving my car, wheeling it around the corner on two wheels.

I asked her, "Are you going too fast? You may have an inner crash." (We will speak of the literal or objective interpretation of the dream in Chapter 10.)

An airplane is different from a car in that a car runs on the ground while a plane flies through the air. So with the symbol of the plane we may ask, What takes you off the ground in your inner life? Is it your imagination, your prayer; is it your spiritual experience? If the plane in your dream is about to crash, then you may ask yourself if your spiritual life, or any of the other ways that it describes, is about to crash.

On the other hand, if you are having a delightful experience of flying without a plane in your dream, you know that it cannot happen in waking life. Therefore, it may suggest fantasy, or a desire to escape from real life. The dream, however, does not condemn, it only reveals. The psalmist said, "How then can you say to me: 'Flee like a bird to your mountain' " (Ps. 11:1b).

There are no absolutes in the interpretation of symbols. In one dream the king of Babylon was represented as the head of a statue, in another he was represented as a great tree. To say that a tree always means a king would be altogether wrong. That is the problem with a dictionary of dream symbols which suggests only one or two possible meanings of a symbol. The meaning must be drawn from the dreamer for each dream, and the meaning of the symbol may be different in the next dream, even though some symbols may be used more commonly for an individual.

There are many symbols used in the dreams and visions of the Bible. There are sheaves, the sun, the moon, the stars, grain, bread, fat and thin cows, grapes, birds, a ladder, barley loaves, a boiling pot, wheels, armor, a belt, a breastplate, feet, a shield, arrows, swords, helmets, dragons, trumpets, seals, bowls, cities, people, and many more. All of these biblical symbols could come in our dreams today, but we must not limit ourselves to those found in the Scriptures any more than Jesus did. Just as He did, we must interpret symbols from the life we are familiar with.

The depths of the ocean often describes the subconscious, or the heart. From there we may bring up good fish in the dream, or sharks. Jesus said, "For out of the overflow of the heart the mouth speaks. The good man brings good things out of the good stored up in him, and the evil man brings evil things out of the evil stored up in him" (Mt. 12:34b-35). I once had the following dream:

> *I was walking on the edge of the ocean rim, like the edge of a bowl. A storm was rising and the water was lapping at my feet. I needed to go on to a little village which was very isolated, yet I did not know whether I was going to make it there and back before the storm became too severe.*

I was in the process of allowing the Lord to examine the depths of my heart, like the ocean. The dream, however, was saying that troubles would be coming. I needed to get to a place of safety, possibly a spiritual fellowship, for I was afraid I might be overwhelmed.

There are other symbols that have general meanings. A square or cube speaks of wholeness, like the New Jerusalem, the city foursquare. A circle is even more complete, which may be pictured by a ring.

> *I once dreamed that I was batting a ball with my children when they were younger. We were in a room too small, for*

the ball would sometimes hit the fancy plastered ceiling and mark it, and sometimes the wall.

The ball symbolized the spiritual matters with which I was dealing. But my room, that is, the room of my heart, was not big enough, and the ceiling not high enough. I needed to enlarge the house of my soul.

Gold, silver, and precious stones are often symbols of value, sometimes of beauty. Each of these symbols, however, may have a unique meaning drawn from the dreamer's own experiences. In the Bible the right side is often the side of authority. In the dream the right side often speak of the conscious side, the mind, while the left speaks of the subconscious, the heart.

We may take the symbol of the river from that which is flowing from the throne of God. It may indeed speak of rivers of living waters at one time; however, at other times the river may represent destruction, as in a flood. It may speak of death, as it does when someone has lost a loved one through drowning. The river may also speak of transportation. Sometimes a river is a border, and a bridge speaks of crossing over into a new land. Always the meaning comes from the dreamer's own association.

A tunnel is a common symbol at a time of depression or great suffering, and a light at the end is a symbol for encouragement. A storm may foreshadow a coming time of trial. An earthquake is used as a symbol in the Scriptures of governments being shaken, and it may be a foretelling that the structures we have depended on are being broken down.

There are symbolic actions as well as objects. If you dream that you are walking along comfortably, but suddenly find that you are about to go over a cliff, it may symbolize a scene about to be played out in your heart. The dream often shows our present condition and what will happen if we continue to go in the same direction. This kind of dream may suggest that although you think everything is fine and you are walking on solid ground, actually there is a cliff ahead and you are about to fall if you do not take heed. It has been suggested that a dream can give us the best possible picture of our present condition.

It is quite common to dream of being unable to find the office or room to which we are going, suggesting that inwardly we are somewhat lost; we cannot find our proper place. Or we may have lost our purse. Since the purse commonly contains money and keys or credit cards, it often suggests that we have lost a treasure of our soul, or our identity. Symbols in dreams are innumerable, and we will illustrate many more as we proceed.

The symbols in a dream are chosen for a very specific purpose. It is therefore necessary first to look at the symbol itself to identify what it is, then what it means. For instance, let us look at the dream of a little boy. He reported,

I was tied to a railroad track, and the train was coming.

It is well to look at the symbol as though we knew absolutely nothing about it, as though we came from Mars. What then is a railroad track? It is a man-made object. It did not grow; therefore, it does not represent a person. It is a piece of steel set in a certain rigid pattern on which the train runs. It is impossible for the boy to change it. The track therefore could represent a rigid pattern of discipline that had been set for the boy in his home. It is a pattern that is impossible for him to change. In school, it may represent the course that was set for the boy and which he cannot change.

Concerning the train, we may ask, What is a locomotive? for that is the first thing the boy would see. Since a locomotive is also a man-made object, it clearly does not represent his teacher. It consists of many pieces of steel made into a huge mobile machine.

Taking that as a base for interpretation, the locomotive may represent a disciplinary act in the home. In the school it could represent the test that the boy sees coming. The test is man-made. In the mind of the boy it is huge and inflexible.

If the train runs over the boy it will surely kill him. But when we look at death in the dream in a later chapter, we will see that this does not speak of a physical, but a psychological death. It would destroy his soul. Therefore, in interpreting symbols it is vital that we look carefully at the symbol itself before trying to interpret its meaning. Grass may be a symbol of new growth, as Jesus used it in one of His parables. A tree, on the other hand, may represent stability. Wood coming from a tree can speak of the building material of the soul that comes from growth. But never is one meaning necessarily the meaning for all dreams. Each symbol must find its meaning from the dreamer. Sometimes the dream is just a confirmation of a decision that we have finally made.

I once dreamed that the Twiddly Styx family left our house, along with other friends, and were on their way to Chicago. They left the man's overcoat at the house. Someone went out to call them or go after them but I realized it was too late.

This dream came after I had spent some time lightly considering doing a bit of tile work in our house. I was not sure I could do it, and played with the idea, but finally decided to venture it. The Styx is a river in the underworld that had to be crossed, and my subconscious was working on the crossing to a new territory. Leaving the overcoat probably meant it was a sign of temporarily leaving my regular profession. I set the tile and it went well.

A dream speaks as frankly as the Bible. It is therefore not uncommon for people to have dreams about the toilet. Some people, after receiving prayer for the healing of memories or confession of sin, have dreamed of filling the stool. They are getting rid of waste.

There are innumerable symbols just as there are objects and experiences. Each of these symbols has its own meaning to the dreamer. We will look at many more of these.

Chapter 8

Animals, Birds, and Fish in Dreams

The Bible uses many animals as symbols. There are snakes, cows, bulls, sheep, lambs, goats, rams, worms, bears, lions, leopards, horses, dragons, and dogs. Among the birds are the dove, the raven, the eagle, the cock, the hen, and the vulture. Sea creatures include the fish and leviathan, which probably is the whale. The spider, the fly, the gnat, and the ant are among the insects we read of.

The lamb and the sheep are the most common. Isaiah vividly describes the Messiah to come as a lamb being led to the slaughter. He is later pictured in the Revelation as the Lamb who became the conqueror. Jesus speaks of His followers as sheep, and He is the Good Shepherd.

In contrast to the meekness of the lamb there are some thirty-five references to the fierceness of the dragon. He is the great serpent finally conquered and cast into the lake of fire. The serpent, or snake, is a significant but paradoxical symbol in the Scriptures. The beguiling serpent in the garden of Eden deceived Eve, which resulted in Adam's fall into sin. Yet the brazen serpent in Moses' day became the symbol of healing, and Jesus pictured Himself as the serpent cursed for all. He also challenged His followers to be wise as serpents. Later we will see how these symbols relate to the snakes in our dreams.

Daniel dreamed of many strange animals. "In my vision at night," he wrote, "...four great beasts, each different from the others, came up out of the sea. The first was like a lion, and it had the wings of an eagle. I watched until its wings were torn off and it was lifted from the ground so that it stood on two feet like a man, and the heart of a man was given to it...a second beast, which looked like a bear...another beast, one that looked like a leopard. And on its back it had four wings like those of a bird...and there before me was a fourth beast—terrifying and frightening and very powerful" (Dan. 7:2-7).

Zechariah the prophet described horses in his vision. "The first chariot had red horses, the second black, the third white, and the fourth dappled—all of them powerful." The angel said, "These are the four spirits of heaven, going out from standing in the presence of the Lord of the whole world" (Zech. 6:2-3,5).

In the apostle John's vision he saw the heads of horses, which he said resembled the "heads of lions, and out of their mouths came fire, smoke, and sulfur" (Rev. 9:17b). Finally there is the "white horse, whose rider is called Faithful and True" (Rev. 19:11). This rider becomes the final conqueror.

In light of the abundance of animal symbolism in the Bible, it is not strange that there should be many animals in our dreams. Like the animals of Daniel's dreams and visions, which represented the nations that were fighting and contending with one another, so the animals in our dreams often picture our emotions or instinctual traits. When the huge animals that charge head-on come in our dreams, they may well symbolize our anger, lust, jealousy, or other such emotions. A woman from a British Commonwealth country reported such a dream. She said:

A man, woman, and child are on the run from someone. They are running through dense bush. They know there is a path there to follow but it is hard to find and very overgrown. Suddenly I become the woman, and Michelle is the child. I do not know who the man is.

Behind us we can hear wolves, and they appear to be gaining on us. We can now see them at the bottom of the hill and I get a real trapped feeling. Michelle goes on up the track and appears to be making it to safety. The man slips away to find a hardware store from which to buy guns. I turn and face the wolves. They are only a few yards away now.

Above my head, in the forest, are several shelves, densely packed with books—there must be thousands. I start throwing the books at the wolves, who by now are almost at my feet. I am frightened, but I know that it is up to me now. I have no one to call on for help, and I realize I must face this myself. The wolves stop at my feet. The books don't bother them, but neither do they attack me. I am a little less frightened. Then I wake up.

You will notice the incongruity of finding book shelves in the forest, but that is only so if you think of it rationally. It is a symbolic dream and must be approached from that perspective. I was not able to find the meaning of the dream as we looked at it together. That does not disturb me. I am only there to help the dreamer find the meaning; so I gave her some suggestions. Soon she came back with the interpretation relating to the setting of her life.

"I think this speaks of my relationship with my mother," she said. "I am questioning (to myself) her values more and more and feeling hounded by her and have recently confronted her a few times when I have openly disagreed with her, something I have never done before. I have recently been throwing a lot of books her way to help her see where I am at, and what I believe in, but I don't think they're going to make her change her values at all."

Suddenly the meaning of the symbols of the wolves and the books became clear, and it was a revealing picture of her family situation. There is more in the dream about the man and the child which we will take up in a later chapter.

I once had a dream of a wolf that had a different symbolic meaning:

I was in the living room of our house. People were sitting on chairs which had been set around the walls of the room. A wolf was edgily circling around the room behind the people. I drove him out of the house and away from it. However, the wolf did not want to go, and the last picture I saw of him he was still looking back at me.

Upon awakening, I knew that the house was not our home. It was instead the house of my soul at that time. This dream came at a time after I had been deeply hurt by someone close to me. I determined, however, that I must forgive this person, but this was difficult because the hurt was so deep and unexpected. I persisted, however, to work at forgiveness when the dream came.

I recognized that the wolf represented a bitterness that had come into my heart because of the hurt. The dream showed me that I was driving it out by offering forgiveness, but that bitterness was still wanting to come back. Furthermore, I remembered that wolves travel in packs, and if the bitterness came back it would come back with a pack of other emotions. Therefore I must proceed with the process of completely forgiving the one who had hurt me—a very timely dream.

It is well to study the habits of animals to understand what they symbolize in dreams. Lower animals will attack any part of the body. More highly developed animals attack more deliberately. Sharks will bite off any part. The cat family and bears will attack from behind, usually the torso area. Primates go for the throat, particularly the jugular vein.

Some animals, such as the fox, the cock, the lion, and the eagle, have common symbolic meanings: the fox with its cunning, the cock with its early-morning call, the lion with its royalty, the eagle as king of the sky. They may have different meanings for each individual and must be checked with each person. Each symbol may mean something different to each person.

An Australian missionary working in a difficult area of that country had the following dream:

I was wandering about the grounds of the base. The grounds looked just like they actually were; however, one corner looked a little like a part of the back of our old house. My children and some others were playing by the fence, made of plain and barbed wire, near a gateway with bushes and trees on the other side of the fence. Where the children were playing was a small box with toys. I saw the box and was concerned that there were redbacks (spiders) in it; so I looked to see not redbacks but a large frog-green spider about ten to fifteen inches in size. I saw it come out of the box and catch a bird and carry it up to its web to kill and eat it. I sent the children away.

I looked around and became aware that the web was over the whole field and was ten to twelve feet above the ground like a heavy net with thick, that is, one-eighth-of-an-inch, strands. This worried me, so I picked up a heavy stick to tear down the web and kill the spider.

As I began tearing down the side of the web I was concerned, almost fearful, of the spider falling on me; even so I continued. Then I saw the spider on the ground, but it was not the whole spider, just a few pieces of its legs. I thought, "This cannot be," but it was; and the bird it had captured was standing in the middle. It had lost nearly all of the feathers off of its wings; however, it had indeed killed the spider and eaten it, losing some feathers in the process.

The missionary recognized that the huge spider represented satan, who had woven a web of intrigue and fear over the mission base. The web was strong. Since a spider web is thinner than a human hair, a strand one-eighth of an inch thick would be impossible for a man to break with his hands.

The little bird was fragile. However, since a bird is able to fly, it often represents that which is above the earth. Here it represented his spiritual life, but sadly it became caught in satan's net of fear and deception. Naturally it seemed impossible for the little bird to defend itself against such an enemy if caught in its web.

The dream told him that the bird not only escaped, but killed the spider; therefore, the dream was God's picture telling him that though his spiritual life appeared so fragile it could kill the spider. Since the bird lost some of its feathers, the dream indicated that this would be a difficult battle. Its flight, due to the loss of feathers, would be impaired, but the bird had won. This was a very encouraging dream for the embattled missionary.

The snake in the garden of Eden is a symbol of deception. Because of that, and because of the fear that many people, especially women, have of snakes, people may jump to the conclusion that the snake is always a symbol of evil in their dreams. It is a symbol of evil many times, but not always.

Jesus said in Matthew 10:16, "Be ye therefore wise as serpents, and harmless as doves" (KJV). Or, as the NIV says, "Be as shrewd as snakes and as innocent as doves." For this reason Jesus preceded His words about the serpent with, "I am sending you out like sheep among wolves." He was saying that they were to be shrewd in carrying their message, for they would be among many dangers.

Many people have dreams of snakes; yet they are aware that snakes are not necessarily always evil. In one dream, the dreamer said:

> *I am surrounded by snakes, and I am not afraid of them (though I am terrified of them in real life); but I know that I must be careful, for they can bite me."*

Sometimes people may be afraid of the snakes in their dreams, for they are afraid of the wisdom they are confronting.

When we face truth that may not agree with past tradition, we may indeed be afraid of it, though that does not make it evil. This agrees with the common psychological concept that the serpent is the symbol of wisdom. However, I believe it is a wisdom that can be perverted. We can use the wisdom that God gives to all the world, but we must be careful that we are not deceived when others want to twist the truth for their own purposes.

On the other hand, the snake is also the symbol of healing. When Israel had sinned by complaining, God allowed poisonous snakes to come among them, and many of the people were bitten and died. Then God told Moses to make a serpent of brass and told him that anyone bitten by a snake could look steadfastly at the brazen serpent and live. The snake even appears on the doctor's caduceus.

The snake was the cursed animal; therefore, Jesus took the snake as a symbol of Himself, for He took the curse of our sins upon Himself when He was put on the cross. He said, "Just as Moses lifted up the snake in the desert, so the Son of Man must be lifted up, that everyone who believes in Him may have eternal life" (Jn. 3:14).

Typically a dog or a puppy comes into a dream as a pet. In Bible days, the dog was a scavenger. Twice the Bible speaks of a dog returning to its vomit (see Prov. 26:11; 2 Pet. 2:22). A connection is often made between a pig and mud, but I learned of another interesting association. In the days of sailing ships, pigs were used as an aid in navigation. When sailors were unsure of directions, they would throw the pig into the ocean, for it would always head north. At landfall it would be butchered for food.

A dream may use any of these figures. The animals frequently speak of our emotions, as the following dream clearly reveals:

Our dog had died. Two of my brothers and I were carrying the dog to a place to bury it. We showed no emotion and seemed to feel no emotion. We carried the dog down into a hole big enough to bury a large dump truck—very deep. Then we walked back out of the hole so we could bury the dog. We felt no emotion toward each other or the dog. We showed no emotion in our face.

"In our family," the dreamer told me, "we learned not to show our emotions, at least not the negative ones. Some of my emotions are buried deep. It is hard for me to let them out. It doesn't feel safe. It wasn't [safe] when I was a child."

Horses are often symbols of power in dreams. We speak of horsepower for our cars. The horse is a symbol of energy, which is symbolized beautifully in this dream:

I see a whole herd of beautiful horses and I'm racing with them. They almost overrun me, but yet I am thrilled for the adventure."

The lion is a great symbol of royalty, used often this way in the Bible and in literature. For a time I was being chased by the cat family, the lion and the tiger. At first I was frightened and ran to hide and escape from the animals. I soon learned an important principle, however: always face your fears. On awaking I faced the lion, and after that the lion became friendly.

In the last of that series of dreams on the cat family, I was walking along and suddenly saw a huge lion coming towards me from behind with great leaps and bounds. I put my elbow out and the lion put his head in my arm. We walked off together. That indicated to me that all the energy in this powerful lion I had been fighting had now become mine, for the lion had become my friend. The emotions of anger, fear, lust, jealousy, and envy have a great deal of God-given energy in them. When we face them and surrender them to God, that energy becomes ours. When I was about to travel into the Soviet Union while it was still a closed land to us, I had the following dream:

> *A huge lion was just outside the front door and was watching the back door. I was afraid to leave the house. Then the lion wanted to come into my little house, but he was afraid of the bear. Finally he came and we became friends.*

Lillie and I had been invited to go into the Soviet Union to teach. Because of the fear of communism instilled in us as children by the many stories we had heard of those who were being persecuted there, we were afraid to go behind the Iron Curtain. We struggled with this fear, knowing the Scripture that said, "Perfect love drives out fear" (1 John 4:18a). We knew that we could apply this verse to our situation, but that was merely good theory until we learned how to put it into practice. Finally we learned to pray for the interrogators, for they were the ones who caused the fear and thrust people into despair.

It was when we had arrived in Helsinki on our way to the Soviet Union that I had this dream. The lion was the Lion of Judah, Christ; the bear was Russian. The dream told me that if I would let the Lion into the area of my fear, I would be protected. And this is exactly what happened. We spent some time in the Soviet Union and had no fear. We never were interrogated.

After that came this dream: I was in a country with a big elephant. It was raising its trunk and seemed to want to charge. Then it deflated and lay down like a cat. The fear was gone.

One of the most beautiful dreams I ever received was of a great lion, which I will use later to illustrate the great challenge of spiritual growth.

A friend brought me the following dream of her mother's mule. She said:

> I am outside my house with my family, but it's not my actual family. The house is beside an ocean. I see a mule, which I know to be my mother's mule, heading out into the ocean. I thought I had had this dream before, so I knew the mule was going to go out into the sea and then drop off the shelf and drown, which is exactly what it did. When I saw the mule going out towards the ocean, I told my mother that it was going to drown. We all ran down to the ocean. Somehow they had dragged it out and were trying to revive it, but I knew it wouldn't work. I watched as my mother hugged the dead mule, with a feeling of saying goodbye to it.

This young woman had recently begun her dream work. She was outside the house that she had been living in, which was beside the ocean, the subconscious. Her family symbolized the parts of her that were now brought into play. The "mother" was that part of her that had brought forth her new life. The "mule" represented her stubbornness, which she had exhibited as a child, but which had to die. Her former self was mourning, saying goodbye to the old stubbornness.

Birds often fly into our dreams. Among them are some common symbols, such as the dove of peace, the black raven with its mysterious evil connotations, the cock as the signal of the morning, the eagle as the king of the birds, the mother hen, and the sparrow with its insignificance but value. Sometimes there is conflict among the emotions.

> *Once I dreamed I was in a cave-shaped room teaching a young bird to fly. I had a string attached to the bird, and it flew a little. But each time it did, a cat lurking nearby in a pool of water would spring at the bird.*[1]

My spiritual life wanted to get free but I had a string on it so that I could control it. Furthermore, the cat, representing my old emotional nature,would spring at the bird. It reminded me of the chorus, "Set my spirit free that I might worship Thee."

A woman once told me of this dream:

> *I had been looking out the window at a forest in winter. About twenty feet in on the left side of the path was a tree whose branches hung over the path. Two owls were sitting on the same branch, one facing toward me, the other with his body forward but head turned to look at the other owl. I held my breath as I noticed that not only were there two owls, but about five or six feet back in a tree on the right side, on a branch overhanging the path, a little man crouched. He looked like a leprechaun, except he was about one and one-half to two feet tall, the same as the owls only much wider. He was dressed in dark clothes with a hat and had big pointed ears.*

This dream was set in the forest, which may represent the mysterious fantasy she was having. To this woman the owls represented something beautiful and free, which she rarely saw. The leprechaun suggested the concentration of her masculinity, small but with big ears. Both the freedom of the owls and her concentrated masculinity needed to be integrated to fulfill her desire to minister to others through gardening and nature work.

A very short dream can have powerful meaning to the dreamer. One man said, *I saw that my leg was very badly inflamed. In fact, I saw the red veins running down my leg. In the next scene I saw my briefcase, with a very poisonous spider sitting on it.*

I asked the man for what purpose he used his leg. He said, "For walking." "Is there something wrong with your walk?" I asked. With that the man saw in the picture what he had denied with his mind, and was deeply affected. He knew that he was wrong, but had reasoned it away. Then with powerful emphasis a second dream showed him that it would affect his work also. The poisonous spider represented an evil thought that had taken hold of him, affecting his "walk" with God. Once he realized the impact it would have on his profession, he immediately turned from the way he was going.

Animals, birds, fish, and insects in our dreams often speak of our emotions or natural instincts. They show us by their pattern of life what is going on within us. Animals in our dreams are less conscious than the people, which we will look at later.

Endnotes

1. Herman Riffel, *Dreams: Wisdom Within* (Shippensburg, PA: Destiny Image, 1990), pp 49,50.

Chapter 9

Children's Dreams

Children's dreams are important, because they often reveal the fears and joys of their hearts. Jesus said, " 'Let the little children come to Me, and do not hinder them, for the kingdom of God belongs to such as these' ...And He took the children in His arms, put His hands on them and blessed them" (Mk. 10:14,16). It is no wonder then that children are full of dreams.

A mother once told that she was praying that her children would stop having nightmares. I said, "That is like praying that they won't hear the fire alarm. That is not a good idea." The children were having these frightening dreams because something was going on in their lives that was causing them. Therefore, the thing to do was to pray and seek the cause of the dreams, such as in the case of the boy who dreamed of being tied to a railroad track and the train was coming. When you remove the cause, the nightmares will stop.

Another mother told me that she and her children had had a delightful time talking about their dreams at the breakfast table. She could join in the happiness revealed by their happy dreams, and when there was a sign of fear in the dream, they would talk and pray about it. Children's dreams are not simply a replay of a recent television show, though dreams may pick up images from a show to illustrate a point. The show may also release fears awakened by it. A friend once told me of this dream:

> *Between the ages of eight and twelve years I often dreamed that I was in the narthex of our church, and I was climbing up the child steps for a drink at the water fountain. As I bent to turn on the water and drink, someone turned it on for me. I would look up into the beautiful face of Jesus and His incredible eyes were full of love and acceptance. He smiled very calmly and gently. It was the antithesis of all that was going on in my life and in my family, which was profoundly difficult.*

A father told me about the frightening dreams his little daughter was having:

> *She saw a man standing at her bedroom window with his outstretched arms. She thought it was her father, but she was frightened. Again the little girl saw Jesus with His outstretched arms at her window. This time she was very frightened because He wanted to grab her.*

With the second dream I knew that this was not a picture of Jesus, but was satan imitating Him. I asked the father about the house in which they were living. He said that the former inhabitants had had seances and evil activities in it. Therefore, we took authority in the name of the Lord Jesus Christ over the evil spirits that still inhabited the house and drove them out. Thereafter the little child ceased having these dreams.

A similar thing happened in the United States. A mother told me that her little girl would not go to sleep unless the lights were left on. She would always be looking up to the corner of the room. As the parents told me of this, I prayed with them and likewise "cleansed" the room. After that the child had no problem sleeping without the light.

A kindly woman working with pediatric cancer patients was very involved in preparing them for death. She shared with me some of the beautiful dreams of these children, showing God's great love and care for them.

My daughter wanted to know if we had our seat belts on, or were we coming or not.

One European boy of five asked for bags to be packed as he was going on an airplane journey. When he died, three people, his mother, his pastor, and his pastor's wife, were given a vision of him ascending into the arms of Jesus.

A ten year old Maori girl, who had a vision a year before she died, was delighted to find that Jesus had brown skin just like her. As she was dying she announced, "He's coming. He's coming in a canoe over the water.

It can be a delightful thing to listen to children's dreams and enjoy feeling the pleasures they find in them. It is also important to be able to discern what is going on in their inner lives in spite of all outward appearances. We must be careful not to burden them with the same rules of interpretation that we might follow as adults, but remain with them on their level of understanding. Their imagination is great and their symbols, though real, may be exaggerated. Nonetheless, we can be helpful to them in both their joys and their troubles.

Chapter 10

The People Who Appear in Dreams

When we dream of people, we are looking into a mirror to see the many parts of ourselves. The dream mirror is like a prism. Just as a prism divides light into many colors, so a dream shows us the many parts of ourselves. Therefore, when we dream of people, we must ask ourselves, "What does each person represent to me?" This is called a subjective dream. The people in such dreams usually reflect those aspects of our inner selves, good or bad, that need to be brought into our consciousness.

Jesus said, "The good man brings good things out of the good stored up in him, and the evil man brings evil things out of the evil stored in him" (Mt. 12:35).

The Bible provides two vivid descriptions of what may be found in the heart of man. In the first one Jesus said, "For from within, out of men's hearts, come evil thoughts, sexual immorality, theft, murder, adultery, greed, malice, deceit, lewdness, envy, slander, arrogance and folly" (Mk. 7:21). In the other description given by the apostle Paul, he writes that if the Holy Spirit is allowed to dwell freely in our hearts, there will be "love, joy, peace, patience, kindness, goodness, faithfulness, gentleness and self-control" (Gal. 5:22).

Jesus often illustrated good and evil in His parables. We find the characters in them to be wise or foolish, sowing good or bad seed. We also find kings and servants, men and women, bridegrooms and wedding guests, Pharisees and priests, robbers and murderers, and many more from all walks of life.

The Subjective Dream

The characters we find in the parables are the same kinds of people we may find in our dreams. On the average, it seems that about ninety-five percent of dreams are subjective; that is, when we dream of other people, they speak to us about ourselves. These people do good and bad things, and often we know who they are. Therefore, to understand the people in our dreams we must ask ourselves, "What does that person represent to me? What is the outstanding characteristic?" Then I will know what part of me that person represents.

One of my earliest discoveries of this principle came to me in a short scene.

I dreamed of a boyhood friend, of whom I had not thought of for a long time.

Immediately I wondered, "Why did I dream of him? He was the most dogmatic person I have ever met." But upon further reflection I realized that at that time I had been dogmatically arguing in a particular situation. I did not even know that there was a dogmatic aspect to my personality. It was hidden in the heart, the subconscious.[1]

I may dream of a president, a king, a gambler, a murderer, a businessman, or a fool and see parts of myself that were hidden in the subconscious but are now revealed by the dream. We are not in total control of the content of our hearts. Often it breaks forth in the most inopportune time and way. Therefore, it is our duty to bring all these parts into consciousness, for we can only surrender to Christ that of which we are conscious.

As we prepare to look at the many people who appear in our dreams, we need to see the many different aspects of ourselves. Sometimes in counseling, when people are unaware of the unconscious expressions of their lives, they think that they are only what they appear to be to themselves. But if they will observe these aspects, they will note that these aspects will manifest themselves involuntarily. Suddenly they will pop up in their associations with family or friends, or even more likely with their enemies. They also manifest themselves in dreams.

A very kindly young woman told me that she thought herself to be a happy-go-lucky kind of person and a people pleaser. These two aspects of her personality were quite evident; therefore, people would often describe her that way. After a while, however, she began to recognize other aspects too. She said that she was an organizer, a planner, and furthermore, she might be called a teacher-perfectionist at times, for she wanted things done perfectly according to her idea of perfection. If they were not done as she wanted, then a bully-controller would appeared. If that failed, there was an aspect that few people ever saw except, unfortunately, her children. It was the angry dog.

After the angry dog had barked, she was remorseful and the soul-searcher would come out. But it was not the one of whom the psalmist spoke, saying, "Search me, O God." Instead it was the voice that judged and condemned her. Then came the hospital patient, who had a pity party and wanted everyone to come to it. If they did not respond, then she began to pout and become a hermit. But this is not what she really wanted to be; rather, she wanted to be the mother hen who would gather everyone under her wings.

What this woman observed about herself could come out in her dreams. She could meet the happy-go-lucky person skipping along and see the people pleaser bowing to everyone. The organizer and perfectionist would act out their parts along with the bully-controller, and the angry dog would be barking. She might see the soul-searcher examining herself, the hospital patient wanting care, and the hermit alone in the desert. Even the mother hen would take her part. All these aspects of her inner self appeared as individual people in her dreams.

That is the work of the dream. It reveals the hidden aspects of our inner selves that we don't see. Though others may see them, we often won't believe what they tell us. The dream, however, accurately reflects these many aspects of ourselves. That is one reason why a dream can be so valuable. God's aim is to make us whole, but in order to become whole these aspects must be recognized and accepted. This is a lifetime process, but often years are wasted because we won't admit that we have so many different aspects of our personalities repressed in our hearts. This is illustrated by one woman's dream. She told me:

At a family reunion Sally was getting ready to go to the shore with many little toddlers. I said I would go along too. I went upstairs to the bedroom to change shoes and clothes. While I was there a lady came up and walked through the room very pleasantly, even walking right through the walls.

"You look familiar," I said. "You are Aunt Susie."

"Yes," she said.

"The one who died in India in World War II," I said.

"Boy, it's great to see you," she said.

Then I went downstairs and whispered in my mom's ear, "Mom, did you see who was here?"

"Yes," Mom said, "I thought she looked familiar."

The dreamer said that Aunt Susie had been the one member of the family she had never known, though she had heard much about. Susie had been a great adventuress and had worked as a military nurse in India. The dream was calling her attention to the adventurer aspect of herself, and as a result she brought it into her conscious life.

Sometimes fighting goes on in our dreams. For example:

I once dreamed that we seemed to be in a civil war. Both camps were near each other. The high officials from the other side came to us.

This speaks of the various aspects of our inner selves warring with one another. We know that these arguments go on within us, and dreams can show us how we can bring peace within.

The Objective Dream

There are occasions when a dream is not speaking symbolically, but is speaking literally about the person we are dreaming about. This is called an objective dream. Objective dreams are comparatively rare in proportion to subjective ones.

We hear of many more objective dreams because they can be easily understood. But, overall, it seems that only about five percent of our dreams are objective. Like the Bible, dreams have much more to show us about ourselves than about what we are to tell others.

There is no foolproof way to tell which is an objective dream and which is subjective, except in hindsight. The safest approach is to first consider the dream to be subjective. If this absolutely does not fit, then consider it objective. I emphasize the importance of trying it out as subjective very thoroughly first, for we are too easily tempted to project our weaknesses and failures onto others.

The most common problem with dreams, a problem that has caused much damage, is people taking subjective dreams and interpreting them as objective dreams. This is a common complaint among Christians. Someone has dreamed about the problems of the pastor or priest, not recognizing that the dream is not speaking about the pastor or priest of the church at all. It is the pastor or priest aspect of his or her own life that has the problem. But it is so much easier to project the problem onto someone else.

There was a woman who had spent some time at a psychiatric hospital, but who had returned home and was not recovering. This woman's friend dreamed that the recovering woman had a demon and told her about it.

This just about put the woman back into the hospital. The dreamer needed to realize that the demon was in her, the part of her represented by the other woman, and not project her problem onto her friend.

If after careful consideration, however, a dream does speak objectively, then we must ask God what to do with it. We are seldom supposed to tell others that we have dreamed about them. First of all, the dream is probably about ourselves. But if it is about another person, we must be careful to listen to what the Spirit of God would tell us to do. Most often it is a call to pray for that person. Sometimes it may be to carry out some ministry. It may also be a confirmation.

A pastor once had a dream in which he saw a house with all its furniture and the yard outside. He had a very good feeling about the house, but had no idea what the dream was telling him. Later he was asked to preach at a church with the possibility of receiving a call to become the pastor. The leaders of the church took him to the house where he was to live. He immediately recognized it as the house in his dream. Because he had felt so good about it in the dream, he knew it was a confirmation to accept the call to that church.

Though there is no absolute way to tell when a dream is objective except by waiting and listening to the Spirit of God, there are some possible hints and clues. When a person dreams of someone to whom he or she is emotionally connected at the time, then the dream may be speaking about that person. For instance, when I dream about my wife, it seldom is about her, but about what she represents to me. It is a subjective dream. However, if a parent is particularly concerned about one child and is deeply disturbed, then the dream may be speaking about that child, though not always.

A friend in a British Commonwealth country once told me about his son, Mike, who had suffered a nervous breakdown. They had found a doctor who believed in holistic healing and through changes in diet and some therapy, Mike's health had improved rapidly. "I had tried to help Mike when he needed it and back off when I thought he didn't," my friend told me, "but I didn't know how much stress he could cope with." One Sunday afternoon my friend fell asleep and had the following dream:

I was at the doctor's office with Mike, and there was a long blue cord tied from me to Mike. The material was made of what was called bias binding, a material I used in England for binding material together. I was aware that it had been put on at the doctor's office. The doctor came out of his office and looked at the cord. Then he said, "He doesn't need this now," and cut it. I looked around the office, and young children were running around free of cords that had been binding them to their parents.

The day after the dream Mike and I were at the doctor's office, and the doctor called me in to talk to me about Mike. He said, "The goal now is for Mike to become more independent."

I said, "I had a dream yesterday afternoon. Would you like to hear it?"

"Yes," he said; so when I told him, he said this confirmed what he felt: that this was the time to encourage Mike to be more independent.

Another clue to an objective dream is that it is much more true to life than an ordinary dream. Such was the case with the pastor dreaming about the house. He saw it exactly as it was. One woman awakened from a nap in which she'd dreamed of a child drowning; she jumped up, ran to the neighbor's house, and saved a child from drowning.

During the War, a woman came to a friend of ours and asked about a dream in which she saw her son in a plane that had been shot down. It had caught fire and crashed. Our friend, sensitive to the Spirit, said, "You had better pray for your son." The woman did and her son was indeed in a plane that was shot down; it caught fire and crashed. He, however, was saved. Very frequently the objective dream is a call for prayer.

When one is "in love," the possibility of projection is greater, so great care needs to be exercised in the interpretation of dreams. Most commonly, however, when we dream of other people, we are dreaming about aspects of our own selves of which we are not yet conscious, though other people may see them clearly. We must pay attention to these aspects as they become known to us and yield them to God for His control.

Endnotes

1. See Matthew 12:34-35; Mark 7:21-22; Galatians 5:22-23.

Chapter 11

Birth and Death in Dreams

Birth and death are spoken of symbolically in dreams, but because this is often not recognized, such dreams are frequently misunderstood. When Jesus said, "You must be born again" (Jn. 3:7), we know that He was not speaking of physical birth, but spiritual. Likewise, when He spoke of losing your life, He was not speaking of a physical death. He said, "For whoever wants to save his life will lose it, but whoever loses his life for Me will save it" (Lk. 9:24).

Birth

In dreams, birth often pictures the birth of a new idea or concept, a new development. Women have sometimes become disturbed because they dreamed that they were pregnant, even though it was not true physically. It may, however, be true psychologically, and they should be thankful. So birth in a dream should be interpreted as encouraging and promising. A woman once told me of this dream:

I was with other people, perhaps in a family situation, and a baby was expected. I think I am having the baby, but I'm not quite sure about that. When the baby arrived there was a lot of activity, and people talking to me, and me talking to others in a room.

Suddenly I, or we, remembered the baby. As I looked I saw in a hard cane chair, not a baby, but a fetus of about six weeks or so. I panicked about it being left, picked it up, stroked it, and wrapped it up, but there was a detachment in the way I felt, as though it wasn't mine. Then I realized the need to feed it, and it immediately began to ravenously suck from my breast. Everyone was pleased.

As the day went on I noticed the baby growing rapidly from the nourishment. By the end of the day, I exclaimed to people, "Look how the baby has grown in one day—it looks nearly three months old." It was really round in the face and head and had a nice rounded body. I was very pleased.

The setting of a dream is so important. At the time of this dream, this woman had been at a conference at which the speaker had said that the listeners should accept themselves as they are, just as God accepts us. This seemed like an idea that did not belong to her, though it may belong to others.

This was such a new idea to her that it did not seem as though it was time to be born yet. The fetus symbolized this. She set the idea aside, as if on a hard cane chair, for it wasn't her idea anyway. Then compassion and acceptance of the idea began. She fed the idea from within her whole self and it responded beautifully. By the end of the day it seemed that the great thought had been hers for a long time. It had been integrated. Women will often dream of little babies that need care.

With a man it may be presented differently. At a critical juncture of my life I had the following dream:

I dreamed that I was pushing a baby carriage with a little infant in it, like I did when our children were little. I was on a dead-end street, however. At the end of the street was a colonial house. I did not stop but wheeled the carriage right up the walls and over the roof. It was steep, and I even lifted the carriage over my head and the baby fell out, but I was able to catch it and go right over the top of the house.

At the time of this dream I had come into some new ideas about the Holy Spirit's work in my life. But I was also pastor of a church that was not willing to accept these ideas; so I was on a dead-end street there. The colonial house signified the very traditional house of my soul. The dream said that I could go over the top of it, even though it might be rough at times, as it subsequently proved to be.

Later on I dreamed that I was responsible for an eleven-year-old girl as we were on a swimming dock in deep water. Suddenly the girl went headfirst into the deep water. I reached out and grabbed the girl by the heel and pulled her out of the water.

The eleven-year-old girl was the baby in the first dream that had grown to that level of maturity. It was the idea for which I was responsible, but had neglected temporarily, and it was in danger of dropping into the unconscious.

This dream showed me that I must take care of the idea, as I did, and it took me around the world several times.

Death and Resurrection dreams

When a person dreams of an actual physical death, it is most commonly a subjective "death and resurrection" dream. Physical death is usually portrayed symbolically in dreams as we shall see later. One woman was not sure what her dream was saying. She told me:

I was in a house. My mother, children, and husband were there also. I was sick and going to die. It was like at any minute my heart would stop and I would be dead. Everyone was just waiting for me to die. I got up and drove to some place wondering if this would be it for me. I remember thinking I wish I would die since everyone is expecting me to, and even waiting for it to happen.

I was driving back and lost control of everything. Thinking this was it, my body stopped but my heart was still going. I couldn't get my hands and arms to move; nothing was moving but my heart. To everyone it appeared I was dead. I was at the hospital with doctors over me deciding if I was dead. I knew I wasn't dead, everything was dark, and if I were dead, I would be seeing light wouldn't I? I would be seeing Jesus, but why was my heart still pumping and the doctors were not noticing it?

This woman was in good physical health and has continued so; however, she was going through a death process in her inner life, after which she was to experience resurrection to new life. The next step is shown in a dream I had after "death" had taken place. I knew the time had come for the burial of an old part of my life. As Paul said,

I was to no longer live, but Christ was to live within me (see Gal. 2:20).

I dreamed that I was driving along looking for a parking place. I came to what I though was such a place but saw that it was a place for burial. I found a parking place and went to the plot where I saw empty stone boxes, like sarcophagi, lying rather irregularly. I went to the one I knew to be mine. Two women were working there. One looked up at me and said, "Six feet and one half inch." I said, "Six feet two inches." It seemed as if it would be difficult to put me into my tomb, so I offered to do it myself.

Next came the death and resurrection dream.

I started walking and saw a car that was used to drive through the earth. I observed the button to push to go down and to go ahead, but wondered how it worked. Then Lillie and I and another man were being driven by this man's wife to the grave. I wondered how the transfer would be made after we were in the grave underground, whether the earth would fall on us or what, and I had a horrible feeling of the car being driven off and being left there.

But when we arrived I stepped out of the car. We were in a place like an underground garage. I walked to a door, like a garage door, and as I went through it I fell and died, but as I died, I knew I was making the transfer. It seemed that I was not quite through the doorway and the door was closing on me; then someone pulled me a little farther. As soon as I hit the ground I got up and was ready to step into the car I had seen before, which was coming down through the earth for me and the others in the car.

I stepped in and we started off through the earth. We stopped briefly in a place like an underground motel, and

I saw three or four women and a man in the lobby. As I spoke to them, one of the women said that she was Presbyterian, one Methodist, and one Baptist. They had wonderful smiles on their faces, though they also looked as if they had died. Then we left.

This dream came as I began my serious dream work and began speaking about my inner self in the death and resurrection process. It suggested that my ministry would not be in the denominational structure, but among many denominations, which it has been for the last twenty-five years.

Dreams of Actual Physical Death

Abraham Lincoln dreamed of his actual physical death in symbolic fashion as he dreamed of caskets. Often people are greatly comforted when they dream symbolically of death as Lincoln did. A very good doctor friend of ours wrote us of such comfort at the death of her husband, Glyn. She said:

Our cell group consists of three couples: Lynne and Bob (he is over six feet tall), Carol and Stan (he is about five feet eight and a neurosurgeon), and Glyn and me (Glyn is about five feet ten inches). During the night of sleep Lynne dreamed.

She saw the six of us in the cell group visiting together, each of us was clearly identifiable. Glyn, however was the largest and tallest and strongest and healthiest of the group. He was laughing and said, "Oh! I thought I'd died," and laughed as if that were not so.

Another friend found great comfort in a dream that occurred during Christmas time a few weeks after the death of her father:

The setting was a hillside cemetery in winter: a bare tree, cold, windy, cloudy. A mutilated coffin is partially above ground. I remembered that the coffin had been beautiful at the wake and funeral; polished to a high gloss, beautifully shaped and a color of reddish brown. Now it was scraped; the finish gone and the wood beginning to rot. The lid was afar and I could see my father.

Contrary to the condition of the coffin, father was not touched by decay. He looked as well as when I last saw his body at the wake. I marveled and felt a peace. The rotted coffin did not disturb me. I feel the Lord was telling me to stop seeing my father as rotting in his grave, that he is whole with Christ.

A woman in her eighties dreamed of her own death. We all thought it was imminent, but she lived on for several more years. It was nevertheless an encouraging dream to her.

I was walking along what seemed a long wharf. At the end of it was a river, or water, and a large ship, or so it seemed. As I looked ahead I could faintly see my mother and father standing on this ship. They seemed to be smiling as I slowly walked towards it. Then two boys came running to meet me, laughing and saying, "Oh, Lillian, we are so glad you are coming." Those two boys looked to be ten or twelve years old.

I was a young girl again and was so happy to see them. They were my two brothers, Russell and Lloyd. Both have been dead for several years. They ran up to me and threw their arms around me. In the midst of my excitement they said, "We are all waiting for you," and we all ran toward the ship. Then I awoke.

The appearance of loved ones who have gone before is often a great encouragement. However, sometimes a dream also pictures the loneliness of the one left behind. The following is an example:

I dreamed that I was walking down a slight slope and realized that Bill, my husband was walking beside me. Two others were walking in front of me. I knew that he didn't belong to me anymore, but my leg brushed against his leg while walking, and I thought I wanted him back so very badly. I thought maybe I could just have him with me for a while.

Then the dream shifted and I was in bed. I realized he was in the bed too, and I turned over to just put my arm around him and maybe put my head on his shoulder. I woke up feeling all over the bed and finding it empty and said out loud as I woke up, "Oh, I have been alone so long."

Since most dreams are symbolic and are therefore subjective, it is important that we do not take the dreams that speak specifically about death as necessarily meaning physical death. Most often they symbolize the death and resurrection of which Jesus spoke. There are dreams, however, that speak of impending physical death, often to prepare the person for death itself, or to avoid the cause of it. Once, when a very heavy schedule had been set up for me in Australia and New Zealand, I became totally exhausted. Then I had the following dreams in two successive days that gave me warning, and I asked that one of my speaking engagements be canceled.

In the first dream, I went to a plane that had landed. I talked to the pilot, but he could not answer. I soon found that he was in a coma. In the second, I was on a lower floor of a hospital. A team of doctors and nurses came into the room where there were four elderly patients being sustained by life support. The team came with the decision to take the life support away. A nurse went to one bed and disconnected the life support from one man. He reacted by coming to and sitting up, whereupon I awakened.

There was a delightful ending to one experience I had concerning possible danger or death that came through a dream. While in New Zealand I was invited to go white-water rafting on one of the turbulent rivers. Though I had a Huckleberry Finn life in my youth on a river in California, I had never gone white-water rafting. I was sixty-seven years old and did not want to miss this experience.

The river had a twelve foot drop on number five rapids. I was excited but Lillie was concerned. She thought that she may not be able to dissuade me from going, and wondered what she could do. Then she had an idea. Since she knew that I believed in dreams, she asked God to give me a dream to warn me of the danger. What happened was exciting! She had a dream that told her not to be afraid. I ended up having a great experience! Had there been an actual danger, however, the dream would have warned me, for dreams are reliable. We only need to learn the basic principles of interpretation.

Chapter 12

The Way to Wholeness

God's ultimate purpose of our dreams is to bring us to wholeness. Whether the dreamer is a believer or an unbeliever, whether Christian or pagan, the purpose remains the same. God speaks to us where we are and leads us further. It is no wonder that before the Gulf War, Saddam Hussein dreamed that Mohammed spoke to him and told him that his guns were pointing the wrong way. God uses whatever means mankind will receive to relate to him.

God's purpose is to reach the heart and speak to the true self. There are many obstacles in the way, however. We must deal with each of these obstacles revealed in the dream and clear them out of the way. I have drawn a diagram of the soul as revealed by a dream, with a "map" of the route that we will take.

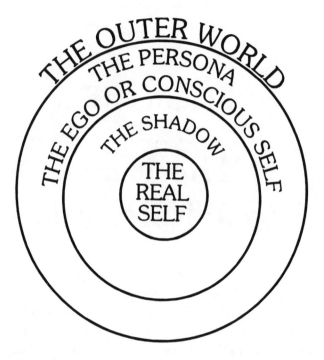

We all have to relate to the outer world around us. We do that with the mask or persona that we put on to protect ourselves. Our life is directed by the ego, which is the conscious part of us. Jesus differentiated the ego from that which is deeper within. He said, "Out of the overflow of the heart the mouth speaks. The good man brings good things out of the good stored up in him, and the evil man brings evil things out of the evil stored up in him" (Mt. 12:34b-35).

We need to look at the various aspects of ourselves that need to be brought into consciousness, and then yield them to God. What is still in the heart or unconscious may spring forth without our conscious control. We must face those things and deal with them before we can go on to discover the real self. It is to the real self that God can speak.

In the life of Jacob we see this pattern illustrated. Jacob was fighting the battle between the ego and the true self. Jesus said, "Whoever wants to save his life will lose it, but whoever loses his life for Me will save it. What good is it for a man to gain the whole world, and yet lose or forfeit his very self?" (Lk. 9:24-25).

The outer world for Jacob was primarily his adjustment to his older twin brother, who possessed the birthright and blessing of his father. Jacob was the favorite of his mother, but Esau was favored by his father. Later Jacob's struggle revolved around the world of Laban, the father of his two wives and owner of all the land and herds.

Jacob put on the mask of being a gracious friend in order to buy his brother with a bowl of soup while he was famished. With his mother's help he put on goatskins, covering his own soft skin to make himself appear like Esau, the hunter. He managed to deceive his father and stole his brother's blessing. All this was done by arranging his persona to meet the circumstances. Then God stepped in to reach for his heart.

Jacob had a dream in which he saw a stairway resting on the earth, with its top reaching into heaven, the angels of God ascending and descending on it. There above it stood the Lord, who said:

I am the Lord, the God of your father Abraham and the God of Isaac. I will give you and your descendants the land on which you are lying. Your descendants will be like the dust of the earth, and you will spread out to the west and to the east, to the north and to the south. All peoples on earth will be blessed through you and your offspring. I am with you and will watch over you wherever you go, and I will bring you back to this land. I will not leave you until I have done what I have promised you. (Genesis 28:13b-15)

Jacob was sure that the Lord was there and said, "How awesome is this place! This is none other than the house of God" (Gen. 28:17b). With his heart he wanted God's blessing, but he had a subtle mind. Up to that time much of Jacob's actions had been influenced by his mother. Having had to flee from his brother, he developed a strong ego to fight against Laban, seeking to steal, if necessary, the flocks of his father-in-law. In this he finally succeeded.

In the process of all this, the "shadow selves" came into play. The thief within him caused him to steal; the deceiver told him to lie; the stubborn one made him hang on; the cunning one gave him the ability to achieve; the patient one waited. But God was still reaching for Jacob's true self.

To do that God arranged for Jacob to have to meet his brother, Esau, whom he had deceived and robbed. But Jacob was still trying to manipulate with his own ego and put on a good persona. None of that would do, however, for Esau was coming to meet him with an army. Jacob sent gifts to his brother. He sent his wives and children ahead, and finally he was left alone. There the angel of God wrestled with him till daybreak.

Jacob finally laid aside all his masks. He surrendered his ego, and his true self expressed itself, taking the blessing that God had promised in the dream, without conniving or using ego power. He surrendered and allowed God to commune with his heart. After that, Jacob started back to the house of God and entered into God's blessing.

An individual seeks to relate to the outer world with his persona, putting on the right mask. Then, with ego strength he seeks to win his battles, but the shadow figures within him tug and pull. When he comes to the end of himself, he surrenders his ego for the true self and finds fulfillment in God.

Through dreams, God is seeking to bring us into wholeness and balance. There are some who through their dreams have learned to fly to great spiritual heights, which is good as long as they also have a good foundation. Others have spent much time with their foundation but have never gotten off the ground. The need for spiritual balance was illustrated by a tragic accident.

Several young people from two families had built a sailboat and taken it out on its maiden voyage. When the parents found that their young people were not at home in the morning, they were alarmed and called the Coast Guard, who found the capsized boat with one young person holding onto it, the other two having drowned. When they checked the sailboat, they found the reason for the tragic accident. The height of the sail was too great for the depth of the keel.

I liken the sail to spiritual experiences and the keel to dreams. There is no limit to the height of our spiritual experiences as long as there is a comparable depth brought about by following our dreams. Sometimes I think that dreams are especially needed by Charismatic and Pentecostal Christians who have found new power by an experience with the Holy Spirit, but who try to keep up appearances by putting on masks. On the other hand, other Christians, and often the psychologists who work with dreams, have a great deal of keel and stay afloat but never soar very high spiritually. Dreams help to bring us into wholeness and balance.

Chapter 13

The Persona or Mask

The mask, or persona, is what we put on when we don't want to reveal who we really are. The word "persona" comes from the Greek theater, where actors would put on masks to pretend that they were someone else. Jesus had much to say about the personas, or masks, that we put on, and it is revealed in our dreams.

There is a place for the persona, for we must relate to the world around us. When we are asked, "How are you?" and we say, "Fine," it is the persona speaking. It is proper, for we are usually not expected to tell all about ourselves, nor would it be good. However, if we always put on a mask and always pretend that we actually are what we only appear to be in order delude people, then something is wrong. Jesus said:

Be careful not to do your "acts of righteousness" before men, to be seen by them. If you do, you will have no reward from your Father in heaven. So when you give to the needy, do not announce it with trumpets, as the hypocrites do in the synagogues and on the streets, to be honored by men...And when you pray, do not be like the hypocrites, for they love to pray standing in the synagogues and on the street corners to be seen by men...When you fast, do not look somber as the hypocrites do, for they disfigure their faces to show men they are fasting. (Matthew 6:1-2,5,16)

The key phrase is "before men." The hypocrites put on actions before people to pretend to be what they were not. This was done to the extreme by the Pharisees and scribes, who were the religious keepers of the law. Jesus said:

But do not do what they do, for they do not practice what they preach...Everything they do is done for men to see: They make their phylacteries wide and the tassels on their garments long; they love the place of honor at banquets and the most important seats in the synagogues; they love to be greeted in the marketplaces and to have men call them "Rabbi." (Matthew 23:3b, 5-7)

This speaks especially to many religious practices when people's religiosity is not real, but by legalistic actions they pretend to be what they are not. These hypocritical actions are revealed in dreams. You cannot observe your dreams and remain a phony Christian for long. Dreams will reveal what you are doing and will not allow you to ignore it.

The mask, or persona, is commonly revealed in a dream by the clothes we wear, for we relate to people in many ways by our clothes. We may want to be fit for the occasion or very casual. In a dream we may be "dressed to a tee" or be simply comfortable. Once, after speaking to a group I had this dream:

> *I was speaking to a group (not the same group, but a group similar to the one I was addressing), but I had no shirt on.*

Upon awakening I thought, "How would I feel if I were speaking before a group and did not have a shirt on? I would feel ill at ease or embarrassed." I then wondered what I was ill at ease about. I listened, for the meaning of a dream or a symbol does not come from thinking but from listening; it comes from the heart and not the mind. Suddenly I realized what the dream was revealing. I had been totally unconscious of it.

One person in the group to whom I had been speaking the day before was not accepting what I was teaching. He was quite an intellectual and led me off into an area with which I was not acquainted. This made me feel ill at ease, as though I did not have a shirt on; I was not properly dressed to relate to him. To make myself feel at ease I decided to let that man go off on his little "rabbit trails," but I would stay where I belonged and be comfortable.

Sometimes we will be naked in the dream, which may indicate that we feel exposed; people can see right through us. On the other hand, it may suggest that we are hiding nothing from God. Only the dreamer will know the correct interpretation.

The uniform is often a symbol of the persona. A choir wears a uniform so that no one person will stand out; all are equal. A nurse wears a uniform to be identified as a caregiver at the hospital. A policeman establishes his authority through the uniform he wears.

A young woman of strong character was troubled by the weakness of her husband. He vacillated and could be swayed by almost anyone. The only time he showed authority was when he put on his uniform, for he was a court officer. He had no authority within himself; he had to put it on. All these things may be revealed in a dream by the uniform. The clothing we wear is significant.

I once dreamed that I was being fitted for the length of my new trousers as an author.

I had a new adjustment to make, for I had never been an author before. Shoes often portray our standing or our connection with the earth, our earthiness. Belts holds things together. A hat covers our head, so it may be a protection of our mind or body. Trousers cover our lower body and so speak of the covering for our walk or sexuality. A blouse covers the breast, which is a symbol of femininity.

A woman had a dream about her persona, but she was not worried about it; she accepted things as they came. She told me:

I was in my closet and all of my silk blouses had little holes at the shoulders. They were worn-looking. I was wondering how the holes had gotten there, because they were new. I thought, "Oh, well," and kept looking through the closet. "There's no use getting upset, they were just cloth and the damage is done."

Another dream tells of a woman who is in a store where she can "buy" clothes for her persona. This woman described her dream like this:

I am in a store and notice a tall older gentleman who is retired and looking for something for his wife. A tall, thin, middle-aged woman wearing an ugly beige coat is very upset and frustrated and talking about it very loudly in the store. I am embarrassed for her. She's talking about how she hates her job and everything and that she wishes she could be like that older gentleman, because he can do whatever he wants and it's okay. He then responds to her and tells her he can even forget his name and it's okay.

There was a shadow part of this woman that had a very poor persona (the shabby coat) and did not know how to relate to the world around her. There was also a masculine, creative part that was comfortable with life and could relate well. She needed to listen to that part of her.

The symbols of the armor to fight the spiritual battles are given us in the Scriptures: the belt of truth buckled around the waist, the breastplate of righteousness, the feet fitted with the readiness that comes from the gospel of peace, the shield of faith to extinguish the flaming arrows of the evil one, the helmet of salvation, and the sword of the Spirit (see Eph. 6:13-18).

In dreams, the skin is used at times as another persona, or mask. The skin is the largest organ of the body. It covers and protects us. A noted dermatologist pointed out that the skin gives a very accurate reflection of our emotions; therefore, the skin may do the same thing clothes do in a dream.

The persona is a necessary part of us. It is the covering, like the skin for our body, or like the clothes we wear. It is good as long as it relates to us honestly, and as long as we do not use it to cover up what we don't want to reveal about ourselves, pretending that we are something else.

Chapter 14

The Parable
and the Dream

A dream is in many ways like a parable. We see a great similarity between them. In the Bible, dreams are spoken of as being like a riddle or a parable (see Num. 12:6-8). Just as we see many people participating in parables, so we may see many in action in our dreams.

Jesus pointed out that below the conscious level, in the heart, are many hidden things that we need to have revealed to us. He said:

Your eye is the lamp of your body. When your eyes are good, your whole body also is full of light. But when they are bad, your body also is full of darkness. See to it, then, that the light within you is not darkness. Therefore, if your whole body is full of light, and no part of it dark, it will be completely lighted, as when the light of a lamp shines on you. (Luke 11:34-36)

As we begin to look at the shadow figures in the darkness of our hearts, we will see them also in the parables. Jesus used parables effectively to teach. In fact, "He did not say anything to them without using a parable" (Mt. 13:34). Much of His teaching was composed of illustrations and stories. The parable of the prodigal son is a good example. In it we see various parts of ourselves.

The story begins, "There was a man who had two sons. The younger one said to his father, 'Father, give me my share of the estate.' So he divided his property between them" (Lk. 15:11-12). We remember that not long afterward the younger son squandered his wealth in wild living and had to feed pigs to keep himself alive. Finally he came to his senses and returned to his father, saying, "Father, I have sinned against heaven and against you. I am no longer worthy to be called your son" (v. 21). But the father would not hear of that; instead, he had his servants bring the best robe to put on his son. He placed a ring on the boy's finger and arranged a celebration.

When the older brother heard about it, he was angry and refused to go in, saying, "Look! All these years I've been slaving for you and never disobeyed your orders. Yet you never gave me even a young goat so I could celebrate with my friends. But when this son of yours who has squandered your property with prostitutes comes home, you kill the fattened calf for him" (v. 29-30). The father replied, "But we had to celebrate and be glad, because this brother of yours was dead and is alive again; he was lost and is found" (v. 32).

The prodigal son is a part that some obviously play, though more often people play the part of the older brother. The prodigal knew that he was a son, for he asked for his inheritance and received it. He asked for it at an improper time, for it should not have been given until after the father died. But the son had no patience, nor did he have discipline to use his wealth wisely. He squandered it and then found himself in dire need.

The older brother had not come into true sonship. He said, "Look! All these years I've been slaving for you and never disobeyed your orders." He had lots of discipline but had never believed that he was really a son. He never understood that he could receive his father's blessing freely.

What we see in this parable, we frequently see in dreams. We see that impatient part of us that has asked for "our inheritance" before it is time, but has squandered it like the prodigal. All of us have the prodigal in us to some measure. We know that we are sons or daughters, but we are too impatient to wait for the inheritance. God's clock does not keep time like ours; its hours are slow and long. But when His time does arrive, it brings great rewards.

The critical older brother can be found in many of us too. Perhaps we would never think to ask as much of God as does the prodigal; we think we are unworthy. We slave to earn our rewards. We are like the older brother, who is angry and jealous of the one who asks freely and claims much.

Then there is the father, who loves both sons and wants to reconcile all the family members. This is the fatherly love, which God implants in us and which we are to nurture. This shows us that the shadow figures are not necessarily evil; they are simply neglected and ignored. Some express themselves in evil ways and need to be more yielded to God for His transformation. Some are creative parts that are as yet undiscovered.

Many of us may well see all three of these figures in our dreams from time to time. We would call them shadow figures. They are not in the light, but hidden in the heart until some unexpected remark calls them forth, or until some event beyond what the conscious mind can handle comes about. Then these shadow figures come into the light. Some see them more often than they wish to admit.

The prodigal son who wasted his inheritance had another part, proper discipline, which he had not developed. We might call it the shadow part of the prodigal son, the part that was not in the light of consciousness, but hidden in the heart. In a dream it might be represented by the older brother, or someone like him, who expresses the discipline that the prodigal has completely ignored.

Likewise, the older brother, who had lots of discipline, had a part that he had not developed. It is the part that knows he is a son and is free to claim his inheritance. In a dream it might be represented by the younger brother, or someone like him, who knows he is a son and is free.

Once the prodigal son integrates discipline into his life, he will be whole, well balanced, and will be able to make use of his inheritance. Likewise, when the older brother comes to accept his freedom along with his discipline, he too will be whole. That is what God is seeking to bring about through our dreams.

There is another parable that shows us various shadow parts of ourselves. It is the parable of the good Samaritan. Jesus said:

> *A man was going down from Jerusalem to Jericho, when he fell into the hands of robbers. They stripped him of his clothes, beat him and went away, leaving him half dead.*

A priest happened to be going down the same road, and when he saw the man, he passed by on the other side. So too, a Levite, when he came to the place and saw him, passed by on the other side. But a Samaritan, as he traveled, came where the man was; and when he saw him, he took pity on him. He went to him and bandaged his wounds, pouring on oil and wine. Then he put the man on his own donkey, took him to an inn and took care of him. The next day he took out two silver coins and gave them to the innkeeper. 'Look after him,' he said, 'and when I return, I will reimburse you for any extra expense you may have'. (Luke 10:30-35)

We all have gone down from Jerusalem, the city of praise and worship, to Jericho, with all its evils of trade. This happens as we move from our devotional time with God to the business hour, where we seek to avoid paying all the taxes we owe. On the way we meet the robbers who strip us of our clothes, beat us, and leave us half dead. These are our shadow parts, which criticized us, taking away our good name, saying we are worthless. They chastise us until we are left half dead.

The priest part of us notices what has happened. I remember well when the priest part of me saw my daughter in her distress. I played the part of a good father and pastor and gave her many good clichés which she could easily see right through. In actuality, I passed right on by her saying, "God can help you," not admitting that I could not help her. But then came the Samaritan, the foreigner whom the Jews despised. My "Samaritan" was the truth that existed in psychology in spite of its frequent confusion, for what I had previously seen of it (which was not much), I did not want.

But God used that despised "Samaritan" of psychology to open great areas of truth that the church had neglected. Now I have the opportunity to return the compliment by presenting the spiritual principles involved in psychological counseling to many psychologists, psychiatrists, and lay counselors. Very often, when we are at the end of ourselves and frustrated concerning a problem, the "Samaritan" will come in a dream in the form of someone we had formerly despised.

In the parables we see examples of the shadow parts of ourselves that we have ignored and neglected. In the same way we see these parts also as we meditate on many of the stories of the New Testament. We have the Pharisee in us, who strictly keeps the rules of tradition, but neglects the greater principles of love and compassion. But there is also the reconciling father and the good Samaritan, whom we need to recognize and encourage. We will see each of these in the dreams recorded in the chapters that follow.

Chapter 15

The Shadow Figures in Our Dreams

Now that we have seen the shadow figures in the parables of Jesus, we can look at them in our dreams. These people represent aspects of our personalities that we have neglected or ignored. They are the Samaritans whom we have despised. They cause us trouble; therefore we do not like them. However, God wants us to accept and integrate all of our parts, which He has created.

Over the course of time, innumerable people appear in our dreams. As we first begin to work with our dreams, we may especially dream of a great variety of people. We may think, "These cannot all be parts of me." But usually the people who appear in our dreams are indeed parts of us, though at first we may only recognize them one at a time. Furthermore, they are of all kinds. In our dreams there are people that we never would have expected. However, when we understand the purpose for which they appear, concern will turn into appreciation. We must therefore learn to look at these people from God's perspective.

As we begin to examine our dreams, we must strive to integrate the good in each of these symbols, even the terrible ones, for they all have some good part. The good part of the thief is that he wants something good, though he goes about getting it the wrong way. The liar tries to make things good by twisting the truth. The murderer wants to get rid of evil, but by killing the one he thinks is evil.

When we dream about a thief, we may be seeing that part of us that wants a good thing but is going about obtaining it in the wrong way. If we dream of a murderer, we need to accept the murderer part of us, and be diligent about getting rid of evil, yet not by killing that part of us. Remember that Jesus spoke of violence when He said, "If your right eye causes you to sin, gouge it out and throw it away. It is better for you to lose one part of your body than for your whole body to be thrown into hell. And if your right hand causes you to sin, cut it off and throw it away. It is better for you to lose one part of your body than for your whole body to go into hell" (Mt. 5:29-30). Jesus was speaking of a symbolic gouging and cutting just as dreams do.

The answer, therefore, is not to deny the shadow figures we don't like and push those parts into the unconscious, but to face them and let God redeem them. We face them by admitting that they are part of us. Only then can we bring them into consciousness, for we can only yield to God that of which we are conscious. The process of growth is largely an acceptance of all the shadowy parts of ourselves and integrating them into our lives.

A girl in her puberty years dreamed that she was killing her mother and felt very guilty.

The dream, however, was saying that in the maturing process, as she comes into her own, the mother must symbolically die. The girl needed to come into a new relationship with her mother, not as a child to a mother, but as an adult to an adult. Many men and women in middle age have never yet cut the umbilical cord; they are still tied to their mothers. Sometimes the dream will speak gently, as with the mother and son in the objective dream in Chapter 10, but at other times it will speak violently, for violence is sometimes necessary. I once had a vivid dream of that kind, a nightmare, early in my dream experience.

I dreamed that it was night, and I was alone in the basement of a department store. All the counters were covered with muslin cloths. Suddenly I saw a policeman break into the store. This was illegal. I went to the telephone and called the police headquarters for help. A policewoman came. The policeman and the policewoman faced each other with their guns drawn. Then the scene changed, and I was on the floor of the living room of our home. My mother was standing on the landing of the stairs leading to the second floor. We had our guns pointed at each other. Then I shot and she fell. I awakened with great remorse, for I loved my mother.

At the time of this dream, my son and I were in conflict. He was at the point in his growth where he was demanding certain rights, but I wanted to keep things as they were. Symbolically, it was at night, because things were not altogether clear. Suddenly the old masculine authority figure broke in—the part that would demand obedience. Then the woman, the feminine creative figure, also came with authority.

I was then at my childhood home on the stairway (in the upward learning process). My mother was a peace-loving soul, whom I had tried to emulate. She was on the landing where there was room to turn. My gun was drawn, and I shot the creative, peace-loving part of me. Thankfully, the dream showed me that if I did do that, I would have great remorse. The result was that I backed off the conflict with my son, and it was resolved peacefully.

A very fine Christian woman came to me because she was disturbed about her repeated frightening dreams. She was the sweetest, most gentle and kind woman; yet her dreams were nightmares.

> *"Someone is chasing me," she told me. "It is someone with a thermometer in her hand. I run from one building to the next."*

I asked her who carries a thermometer. She said it was a nurse, and then she suddenly remembered. It reminded her of the nurse with whom she was working. I knew the nurse. She was just as fine a Christian as was the dreamer, but she was of strong character and a well-organized person. Then I explained that it was not the nurse who was chasing her, but what the nurse represented.

It was the strong leadership part of herself that she had been ignoring in order to be sweet and nice. She thought the woman chasing her was going to get her, to do some damage, but that was not the case. The dream was saying that the leadership part of her had been ignored so long that it was pursuing her in order to be integrated so that she could be made whole. She was running from one organization (building) to the next.

When animals or people chase us in our dreams, we tend to think that they are coming to destroy us. That is not usually so. They are seeking to get our attention. When we acknowledge them upon awaking and inquire who they are, there will usually be a friendly, informative response, for we are speaking to an aspect of ourselves. Then, with that information we can proceed to yield that aspect to God and integrate it.

My shadow figures once appeared in an amusing way:

I dreamed that I was in front of a house on a small street. In front of the next house to the right was a Greek woman, and beyond her in front of the third house stood an Italian man. From across the street a man called to me and said, "If I were lonely, I wouldn't come to you; I would go to the Italian." The Greek neighbor said, "If they come and speak first, then I speak." Then we all became involved.

These are all different aspects of the one me. When we dream of ourselves, it represents our ego, the conscious me. The man across the street, a shadow part of me, is speaking to my ego, which said nothing. The man said that he could not find comfort for his loneliness from my ego, but could get it from my Italian shadow figure. The Greek woman represented that aspect of me that speaks only if it is spoken to.

My wife, Lillie, immediately recognized that about me. She well remembers that when we would be riding the train across country, she would go around and get acquainted with people. I would sit in my seat and read, speaking only if I were spoken to. The dream was calling for the Italian shadow to come forth. To me, the Italian represented one who speaks freely with mouth and hands. I realized that I needed to be more free to speak and to be more friendly, which I had to learn by practice, thereby integrating the Italian shadow figure into my life.

As I have said, a dream is like a mirror reflecting the various hidden aspects of our inner selves. One woman described that kind of dream:

I was in a support group of women. We were sitting on the floor in a circle. Someone I didn't know came and picked me up and carried me over to a big mirror on the wall and threw me into it. The mirror shattered, and I was cut and bloodied, but I was not too surprised by this, nor were the other women. It was done rather matter-of-factly. The woman was not malicious, and it felt like it was something that needed to be done. Over to the side was a good man I knew, but he had strong ideas about how people should be and what they should believe. What was done to me did not bother him.

The woman told me the meaning of her dream. She said, "The other people in the support group are parts of me that are helping me to work on issues I need to work on, even though I have resisted some because they are so painful. It seems that I have repressed some things about my past, and I also repress feelings I don't want to feel. The woman who picked me up and threw me into the mirror, where I see myself, is a strong part of me. That part will do whatever is necessary to help me see the real me—and shatter the image of the me who uses repression in order not to know what is too painful (bloody), but is necessary and in the end will turn out to be good.

"The man I saw is a part of me who is judgmental and thinks it is selfish for me to spend so much time working on these issues, because there is so much work that needs to be done for others. He was not upset about what happened to me, because I should not have been spending my time that way anyway."

A voice in a dream is important and needs to be heeded, as we noted with Dr. Gebremedhen in the first chapter. A layman was helping out in a church without a pastor, but was criticized by some in the congregation when he had a very encouraging dream.

The scene was a theater with a stage and curtains down the side allowing access to the stage from the sides. I was on the stage with another person whom I thought was my wife standing in the curtains in a supportive role. The term "Royal Command Performance" was used for the event. It wasn't announced as such, but that is definitely what it was.

Some person asked, "How did he get there without training?"

The voice that replied wasn't a person speaking, as the voice came out of the air, deep and authoritative: "He has been watching and waiting in the wings, pleased to fill in and take part when necessary. That has been his training ground."

The voice that this man heard was evidently the voice of God. A dream like a mirror is the indirect voice of God; however, a voice in a dream may be the direct voice of God, though it sometimes may be the voice of others in a significant way.

We have spoken of many of the shadow figures that seem negative, such as the murderer, thief, liar, out of which we are to extract the positive parts that we have ignored. Often, however, a dream will speak creatively to bring forth an entirely new expression, as it did with me.

Lillie and I have some great personality differences. This was revealed by the way the functions of the personality may be observed. Jesus said, "Love the Lord your God with all your heart and with all your soul and with all your mind and with all your strength" (Mk. 12:30). These attitudes can also be described as intuiting, feeling, thinking, and sensing.[1] I had developed a strong thinking function, rationalizing everything. Lillie's strongest function was sensing, seeing all the details. Sensing was my weakest function and Lillie's strongest.

God often uses the weakest function to do His creative work through us, though we try to do it all though the strongest function, whether it be thinking, feeling, sensing, or intuiting. God surprised me and gave me a new and wonderful creative expression. Here is what happened.

While giving a series of lectures around the world, some missionaries asked me to put some of my material in a book.[2] "I can't write," I said, for even though I had been a pastor for twenty-five years, I don't think I had ever written out an entire sermon; I could get by with notes. When professors from Michigan State University in East Lansing, Michigan, heard my series of lectures, they too asked me to write. Again I said, "I can't write," whereupon they offered to edit the material, an offer I greatly appreciated. But I was still not convinced that I could write.

Then I gave a series of lectures in Kitchener, Ontario, Canada, where Drs. Glyn and Helen Reesor offered me a private apartment for three months if I would write. A businessman offered secretarial help. I finally decided that I must try. However, an author of many books deflated any over-optimism I might have had. He said that secular publishers accept only one manuscript out of every fifteen hundred submitted and that Christian publishers accept only one out of every two hundred fifty.

Nevertheless, in three months I wrote my first book, and two publishers wanted it. I gave it to one, who asked for the rights on a second book. Another publisher offered advance payment on the next book. So what I once thought I couldn't do has now become a great creative strength as I am presently writing my fifth book. But I thought I couldn't write. Why? Because I hate details, which are part of the sensing function. Once I finally faced the fact that I had to work through all the details of writing, rewriting, correcting, and editing, then I could write.

When I dream of Lillie, it most often is speaking of my weakest function, sensing, that has developed greatly in one area, but needs to be applied in other areas. Dreams reveal the weak and neglected areas of our personality in order that we would accept and integrate them into our lives. The greatest physicists are intellectual giants; yet they often get their great creative ideas through intuition, which would seem to be their weakest function. When a dream shows us our shadow figures, it is to bring us into wholeness.

If we do not accept the dark side of our personalities, that is, the shadow figures that are still in the heart, then we are apt to project them onto others. What I do not like about myself I hate in others. Jesus said, "Why do you look at the speck of sawdust in your brother's eye and pay no attention to the plank in your own eye? How can you say to your brother, 'Let me take the speck out of your eye,' when all the time there is a plank in your own eye?" (Mt. 7:3-4).[3]

This is why when we "preach at" others with great emotion about some fault in their life, it is important to look within ourselves and see if we are not simply seeing the "speck" in their eye that reminds us of the "plank" we hate in our own eye. What we don't like about ourselves we often project on others. In our country, when white people dream of blacks, they are often dreaming of an unknown aspect of their own self. I learned that this is also true when blacks dream of whites. That is because in general we do not really know each other.

This kind of projection often happens among people and nations. When we were in Switzerland, a referendum was being held about allowing foreigners to remain in the country. At the time, Switzerland had about five million citizens and one million foreigners. The foreigners were mostly Italians working in shops and factories.

On a television interview, a Swiss man from the German-speaking part of the country was asked why he did not like the Italians. "They sing while they work," answered the Swiss man. No serious worker of German background would sing at his work. What he did not like about himself—being too serious—he projected on the "foreigner." Every country has its minority that receives the projections of the majority. Dreams can reveal such projections.

If we will work at it, gradually, one by one, we will be able to lay aside our masks, integrate our shadow figures, and become real. George MacDonald described a young man who had gathered shining armor with great pride but who failed miserably in battle. What was worse, there was always a dark shadow following him. He was thrown into prison, and when he finally got out, this is what he said:

> "Now it was ill walking in my heavy armor, and besides I had now no right to the golden spurs and the resplendent mail, fitly dulled with neglect. I might do for a squire, but I honoured knighthood too highly to call myself any longer one of the noble brotherhood. I stripped off all my armour, piled it under the tree...Then first I knew the delight of being lowly, of saying to myself, 'I am what I am, nothing more. I have failed.'

> "I said, 'I have lost myself—would it have been my shadow.' I looked around, the shadow was nowhere to be seen. Ere long, I learned that it was not myself, but only my shadow, that I had lost. I learned that it is better, a thousand-fold, for a proud man to fall and be humbled, than to hold up his head in his pride and fancied innocence. I learned that he that will be a hero, will barely be a man;—he [who] will be nothing but a doer of his work, is sure of his manhood."[4]

With the laying down of the mask and the integration of the shadow, the dreamer will soon be ready for the wedding, which will be pictured in his dream as a delightful anticipation.

Endnotes

1. These functions are more fully developed in my series of lectures entitled "Spiritual Principles Involved in Psychological Counseling."

2. The lecture series is contained in my book and tapes *Christian Maturity and the Spirit's Power.* They may be obtained from the author at 2015 Stone Ridge Ln., Villanova, PA 19085.

3. See the lecture on "Projection" in the series of lectures on "Spiritual Principles Involved in Psychological Counseling."

4. George MacDonald, *Phantastes* (Grand Rapids, MI: Wm. B. Erdmans, 1981), pp. 165-166.

Chapter 16

The Masculine and Feminine in Dreams

When men dream of women and women dream of men, we see an interesting principle being expressed. The dreams seem to be seeking to bring into balance the masculine and feminine traits. Being created in the image of God, both genders have masculine and feminine traits within them. This is because God has both traits.

"God created man in His own image, in the image of God He created him; male and female He created them" (Gen. 1:27). One of the names of God is "The Breasted One." [1] We are not speaking here of a female god or goddess, but rather the traits of God, and mankind made in His image.

---

1. The Hebrew Phrase *El Shaddai* is usually translated Almighty God. It is found 218 times in the Bible. *El* signifies *Strong One* and *shaddai* means the Breasted One. This is according to *Dake's Annotated Reference Bible* by Finis Jennings Dake, 1963, page 14.

The masculine traits are generally authority, logic, abstract thought, determination, and goal setting. The feminine traits are generally creativity, receptivity, relationships, symbolic thought, gentleness, and unconditional love. We can see all these traits in God.

The masculine traits are normally dominant in man and the feminine traits dominant in woman. The man usually wears the masculine traits on the outside, and the feminine on the inside, in the heart or the unconscious area. The woman usually wears the feminine traits on the outside, and the masculine traits on the inside.

If the man has only masculine traits (all macho), he will be strong but cruel. An example of that kind of man is Joab, who served as King David's commander and who was a great general; yet he murdered two generals who might have taken his place (see 1 Kings 2:5). The man who is too feminine, on the other hand, is often extremely sensitive and touchy. King David had both the masculine and the feminine qualities. He was a great soldier and knew how to command his troops, yet he showed much sensitivity in weeping for his son, who had desperately tried to dethrone him (see 2 Sam. 19). The man who is in balance is strong but gentle, characteristics often seen in David's life and of course in the life of Jesus.

The woman who is too masculine will be argumentative, but the arguments will be hollow and dogmatic. If she is too feminine she will be sweet, but there will be nothing to her. The woman who is in balance will have dominant feminine characteristics on the outside but great strength within, like the great women of history. She will be like Esther, a beauty queen on the one hand, but on the other hand showing great inner strength in risking her life for her nation. A description of such a balanced woman can be found in Proverbs 31:10-31.

When a woman dreams about the masculine traits in a real man, it may take the form of a father, a lover, a brother, a teacher, an artist, a philosopher, a scholar, a carpenter, or a sailor. Inasmuch as dreams are always seeking to bring us into wholeness, it may be showing the woman that she needs to integrate some masculine qualities into her life. In the dream of the woman and the wolves described in Chapter 8, the man who went to the hardware store to buy a shotgun was the masculine authority, a part of herself that she needed to recognize. In South America a woman told Lillie her dream. She said:

I dreamed that one of the primitive men of the jungle keeps coming to me. I send him away, but he keeps coming back.

Lillie asked the woman about her life. She was a missionary, and she and her husband had several children. They worked with primitive people, and her husband often had to go to visit the tribe in the jungle. Lillie asked, "Who takes care of the discipline in the home?"

"My husband does," she said.

"Who takes care of it when your husband is away?"

"I wait until my husband comes back," she said.

"It looks like there is a masculine part of you, which is still very primitive, that you need to integrate so that you can take the initiative in discipline when needed," Lillie suggested.

A man may dream of a wife, a lover, a friend, a nurse, a helper, an artist, or a queen. Many women may come into his dreams, all showing him aspects of his feminine, creative side. Gradually they may narrow down to one beautiful woman who represents to the man the sum of all femininity.

Early in my dream experience I dreamed of a despicable woman. I wanted no part of her.

My counselor reminded me that this was a picture of the old feminine part that had tried to run my life. As I progressed in understanding myself and my need for development,

I dreamed of a beautiful woman, the most beautiful woman I had ever seen, standing before a castle.

That was a picture of my true feminine trait standing before the house of my soul.

One man told me the following dream:

I was leading a cow into a barn. The cow had two horns on the left side of its head which were turned backwards. It was a milk cow. Suddenly this cow said, "We don't have to obey his orders" (meaning mine). It began to push me around.

In this case the cow represented the feminine trait in the man. He had the impression that he should not allow the feminine side of him to push him around. He had been raised to be very "sweet" and to never hurt anyone. But this training had left him without proper aggressiveness when needed. Now he was beginning to know himself and allow the masculine authority to be exercised.

Often the most misunderstood dreams are the sexual ones. The problem is that we interpret them literally, forgetting that dreams speak a symbolic language, as God so frequently does in the Scriptures. Dreams communicate to us in a picturesque and powerful language, but must not be interpreted literally.

Hear how God speaks to Israel:

You trusted in your beauty and used your fame to become a prostitute. You lavished your favors on anyone who passed by and your beauty became his. You took some of your garments to make gaudy high places, where you carried on your prostitution...You engaged in prostitution with the Assyrian too, because you were insatiable; and even after that, you still were not satisfied. Then you increased your promiscuity to include Babylonia, a land of merchants, but even with this you were not satisfied. (Ezekiel 16:15-16a, 28-29)

Just as God spoke symbolically to Israel, so dreams speak symbolically to us. When these kinds of sexual dreams are taken literally they can bring much false guilt. There are dreams that speak of lust, but they commonly do so by picturing animals charging or pursuing people. On the other hand, the sexual dreams of which I am speaking are positive, speaking of the call to integrate the masculine qualities in the woman and the feminine qualities in the man. A fine, mature Christian woman gave me permission to quote the following dream:

I was getting ready for bed. I was aware of a man nearby and other people more in the shadows. My impression of the man was that he was somewhat effeminate and he was often near me, though not always visible. I remember thinking, "I know I would not want to belong to, marry, or be with him because he's not my idea of a real man."

I got into bed and wasn't there long till the man got into bed beside me. My back was turned toward him. I wasn't afraid of him. He was passive. Then he turned to a bedside table near him and lit a candle, which gave off a lovely soft light and had a faint pleasing fragrance. Suddenly, my opinion changed about the man. I thought, "He's not effeminate at all, just thoughtful and sensitive."

Then I wanted to belong to, marry, and be intimate with him more than anything. I turned to him, and we embraced just as naturally as if we were meant for each other. He had a big smile on his face when I first turned to him, and he said as he held out his arms to me, "I've been waiting for you for a long time." We were both very happy and I hated to wake up.

When a woman tells this kind of dream to her husband or pastor and it is taken literally, it is easy to see what trouble may be caused. But in working with many upright and honest people who come to me disturbed about their dreams, I have found repeatedly that they are not lustful dreams. Instead they are creative and valuable.

The woman above, who dared to tell me her dream, was a well-balanced, deeply spiritual woman with great maturity. Furthermore, she had an unusually fine husband whom she trusted to make many decisions for their lives. He was a businessman at that time and was being sent away by his company to other countries for a week or two at a time. She knew that she must begin to make some decisions herself, but she did not want to be argumentative or appear mannish.

In the dream the man approaches her in her bed, the place of privacy and creative relationship. But this man did not appear "macho" and mannish; rather he seemed as if he did not have the qualities she thought she would have if she accepted the masculine traits. But when he showed signs of sensitivity instead of mannishness, her mind was changed. That was the kind of masculinity she could accept in her heart.

Her whole being had been longing for wholeness, but there was a masculine quality that was lacking. Now she said that she would like to marry and be intimate with him. Often the dream will speak of the sexual act. However, we must remember that the sexual act is primarily a creative act, meant to bring forth life. The dream was saying that she desired a creative relationship with the masculine, leading, authoritative part of her that would bring new life.

Men often dream of women who are wooing or enticing them. That, too, is a call for a creative relationship with the feminine traits. The feminine part of the man is the creative part, as is the masculine part of the woman. God wants to bring all parts of us into conscious relationship with him—that is, into wholeness.

Chapter 17

The Lion's Challenge to Healing

One of the greatest dreams I ever heard came from a man who was in his eighties and lived in a retirement home in one of the British Commonwealth countries. It came as a challenge to a ministry of healing even at that age.

Often the setting of a dream is found in the immediate circumstances of life. Sometimes, however, the setting is found in childhood. This friend described a setting to his dream that went back sixty years. "Leaving England at age twenty two," he said, "I spent the next ten years serving in the Palestine Police with War Service (an armed constabulary) intervening as Chief Inspector of the Food Ministry. During these years I experienced the horror of racial strife, armed terrorism, bombing, assassinations, etc. I have been called upon to view legal hangings, quite illegal shootings of prisoners, and maltreatment of the wounded. I lost many friends by assassination or in bomb outrages.

127

"I experienced a charmed life during the war, with a price on my head (dead or alive), and was miraculously preserved when I quelled a mutiny single-handed. Instead of rendering me resentful, the net result of my experience was to engender a compassion for the sick and wounded, whether friend or foe."

The dreamer then told of his immediate setting. "At this time I was prayerfully seeking a ministry of caring and healing to utilize my study of herbal and naturopath medicine"—a great goal for his age. Here is his dream:

The place is India, but unrecognizable except for jungle and subject matter. One warm and ideal afternoon I set out on a walk, having nothing in my hand or on my person. The scene before me was a well-cut grass field stretching maybe one hundred yards or so up to the jungle, which consisted of small trees of a uniform height, all very strongly intertwined in the top branches. I walked gently and in deep thought, not on the grass, but on a narrow path ankle-deep in fine dust.

It is apparent from the dream that his soul was in a comfortable position and at rest. The scene of the well-cut grass around him suggests that he was caring for his emotional or spiritual growth at that time. However, beyond the immediate setting of his inner life was a jungle. While the grass may suggest new growth, the trees represent more maturity.

This jungle was a dark, unknown, undisciplined place where wild animals roamed, a part of his life that he had never entered. Apparently the jungle part of his life caught his attention; he noted that the trees were intertwined, that the growth there was tangled. He was in deep thought now. The path was ankle-deep in dust, made not by man but by animals. His emotions had run into the jungle of his life many times, but consciously he had never entered it.

After some moments, I felt a sense of well-being and exhilaration and looking towards the trees, to my amazement, saw a huge lion gradually drawing closer, as our paths would intersect. I somehow elected to keep on my way and face the situation, hardly knowing why.

This dream has an introduction, which we have already considered, a story, and a conclusion or solution. In the story line the dreamer is feeling exhilarated, but gets a shock and surprise as he sees the huge lion. Here is the center of the story.

What did the lion represent? It was huge with a large, black mane. We might guess that it represented one of the man's dangerous emotions. The man was facing it, probably expecting an attack. But the lion, whatever it represented, rolled over and asked for help. This is where we must not leave the symbol to a guess.

In the Bible the lion is represented by two figures of opposite qualities. One is "the Lion of the tribe of Judah" (Rev. 5:5), who is Christ; the other is, "Your enemy the devil [who] prowls around like a roaring lion looking for someone to devour" (1 Pet. 5:8). I asked the dreamer which person the lion symbolized, for the dreamer is the final authority on the meaning of the symbols of his dream. There was no question in the dreamer's mind. The lion was Christ, the Lion of Judah. The man went on to say:

I saw as the lion approached that he had a terrible limp on his left forepaw; also his size was phenomenal, and he had a huge black mane. We faced each other some five yards apart and to my surprise he sat down for a few minutes, then rolled over on his back like a huge, playful dog. I saw a forepaw extended towards me and knew that he was asking for aid, so I advanced somewhat diffidently and extended my hand, lifting the wounded paw and seeing its pitiful condition, so swollen and having a big black something in the pad.

If the lion represented Christ, we may ask why the lion was wounded. The immediate response might be because Christ was wounded for our sins. That is true, but this lion represented the Christ who dwelled within the dreamer. How was the dreamer wounded? For the answer we look back to his youth. When he saw all the terrorism, bombings, and assassinations, his emotions were scarred. This left a jungle hidden away in his heart, which had never been healed. The challenge he faced was this: if he wanted to heal others, then he first had to be healed.

I felt all my pockets, and only found a handkerchief. The second time I searched, a miracle occurred, and I found a penknife (in fact the one my father had given me when I was seven years old). At once I got to work with a probe and extracted a very large tropical thorn. The lion at once jumped up and I retired, wondering what he intended to do. With great dignity he slowly advanced and, like a friendly dog in passing, rubbed his head against my thigh, nearly knocking me over in his enthusiasm. I braced my legs to stand the strain; in all, this act was repeated three times.

At what risk would one take the thorn out of the paw of a lion? Undoubtedly, at the risk of one's life. Is not that what Jesus said? "Whoever wants to save his life will lose it, but whoever loses his life for me will find it" (Mt. 16:25). That is frightening to one's ego, and that is what the dreamer faced. He could either save his ego and comfortably retire, or die to the old self and find a healing ministry.

To take the thorn from the paw of the lion he needed an instrument. At first he found only a handkerchief, perhaps to wipe his brow. That is what often happens when we face a challenge. We do not think we have the tools we need. A more thorough search produced a penknife. What is a penknife to a huge lion?

Again we might guess what the penknife represented, but the answer must come from the dreamer. I asked him what he received from his father when he was seven years old. He said, "I received wonderful training from my father." It looked so small, like the penknife, but the dream was saying that with it he could take out the thorn.

It was not without a great risk—that risk to reputation. Our ego wants to keep the status quo. In fact, someone has defined the ego as "our present way of thinking." That must always be risked to find the true self.

When the lion jumped up, the man retired, wondering what would happen. We wonder what will happen when we take the risk of obedience. But the symbolic picture of the lion rubbing his thigh is beautiful; it would take many words to describe it. Three times it was done, signifying Christ's great appreciation of the man's willingness to face the lion and heal the wound.

The lion returned and sat facing me from about two yards, opening his mouth and roaring. I could see he had a broken and blackened incisor tooth in the bottom jaw,

131

which was terribly swollen. It seemed obvious to me that I must act as a dentist, and I knew I needed forceps.

Now the dreamer was faced with a second challenge. Joseph said to Pharaoh, "The reason the dream was given to Pharaoh in two forms is that the matter has been firmly decided by God, and God will do it soon" (Gen. 41:32). That principle may apply here also. God was showing him that what the dream was saying could really happen if the dreamer accepted the challenge.

At what risk does a person reach into the jaw of a lion to take out a tooth? Surely it is at the risk of terrible death. That, too, is emphasized. Neither the promise nor the risk is minimized. The dreamer decided that he needed to take out the tooth. We'll see what God decided was needed.

At this time a lady (whom I knew from a Bible study group) appeared and stood by me saying nothing: she had an airways bag on her shoulder and turned so that I could see it more clearly. The bag had a red cross on it and in fact was a first aid kit in which I found a pair of pincers (such as those used to take tacks out of carpet).

Here the dream gave very specific directions as to how to do the job. First of all, it is the lady who carried the instrument. The dream was saying that it was the feminine part of him, not the masculine, rational, aggressive part, that could help. It is in the creative, gentle, and receptive part of him that he would find the tool.

The lady had an airways bag, suggesting air travel, or perhaps a spiritual flight. So the tool was carried in the spiritual part of him. Furthermore, the bag had a red cross on it, suggesting healing. It was clearly marked by the blood and the cross, so he was not to use a tool without that mark. It was a first-aid kit, suggesting that it was in the part of him that already had done a little "first aid" kind of healing.

There he found a pair of pincers used to take out tacks. God seems to delight in using small tools to do great works. We are reminded of the four loaves and two fishes to feed the five thousand men, and the seven little loaves to feed the four thousand.

God chose the foolish things of the world to shame the wise; God chose the weak things of the world to shame the strong. He chose the lowly things of this world and the despised things—and the things that are not—to nullify the things that are, so that no one may boast before Him. (1 Corinthians 1:27-29)

Now a mammoth struggle took place, and I finally pulled out the offending tooth, accompanied by deafening roars of pain from the lion. I returned at speed, and again he came three times and rubbed that great head on my thigh. Finally a huge rough tongue came out, and he licked the back of my hand and bounded off across the grass into the jungle.

The victories of the Lord are not won without a struggle and a cost. It is painful to go through the process of obtaining the healing of old wounds. We always wonder what will happen, as the dreamer did. "I retired at speed." We are afraid that God is going to kill us after all, forgetting that this kind of death leads to the resurrection of new life. Then there is the great appreciation expressed symbolically by the rubbing of the thigh and the licking of the hand.

Society often gives up on a person in his eighties. What can be expected of one at that age? God sees all the possibilities and knows exactly what the person is capable of doing. That is why the dream is so encouraging.

"You can do it!" the dream is saying.

Chapter 18

The "Aha!" Moment

Dreams have two interesting figures that appear with unusual frequence: the wise old man and the wise old woman. These figures usually appear to give special insight, or to provide the answer to some problem on which we are working.

In the dream we may be walking along and meet a man or woman who speaks to us and gives us surprising information or insight. Often a man will meet a wise old man in his dream and a woman will meet a wise old woman, but that is not always so. What is common is that the wise man or woman is a person from whom we do not expect such wisdom.

In the Scriptures we find several illustrations of this principle. Abraham received a surprising visit from three men, who promised him that his child was finally to be born. The three men proved to be two angels and the angel of the Lord (see Gen. 18).

A wise man also visited Gideon. He sat down under the oak while Gideon was threshing wheat and said, "The Lord is with you, mighty warrior." When Gideon argued with him, he said, "Go in the strength you have and save Israel" (Judg. 6:12b, 14b). This gave Gideon great courage. The man proved to be the angel of the Lord.

Wisdom often comes in a disguise. After His resurrection, Jesus appeared to Mary as a gardener (see Jn. 20). To Cleopas and his companion, Jesus appeared as one of the people and joined in their conversation. When He was recognized as He broke bread with them, they were overjoyed and their lives were changed (see Lk. 24). Great wisdom often comes in ordinary dress. A woman brought me a delightful dream illustrating this idea:

> *I am standing in a small, lush valley, and on my right, coming over the crest of the hill, comes a figure. It seems he is a wise old sage—he looks and dresses like one of the shepherds of the nativity scene. He is somewhat stooped over from age and hard work. He is smiling and has a twinkle in his eye. He carries a staff, and at first glance I think it is the medical staff, but when I look again it is a stick with a roll of toilet paper stuck on top of it. Some of the toilet paper has unrolled forming a long ribbon that is blowing in the wind.*

The woman explained the dream to me this way: "In the past I have taken my personal spiritual growth very seriously. Even though spiritual growth is serious, I can have fun. The shepherd has a twinkle in his eye. The staff in his hand is not poetic and profound, but practical. There is some wastefulness in my life that I need to clean up and

I have the toilet paper (wisdom) to do it. Personal growth can be fun and light-hearted. I can trust the wisdom (God-given) in myself to do what I need to do. This is the wise old man in the dream, providing practical wisdom."

I had a simple dream of wisdom coming in royal fashion.

I dreamed that an old king of one of the Scandinavian countries came towards me, and Mark said, "He knows more than you do." In jest I replied, "That is surprising, and especially for someone to say so."

This dream said that the wise, old, royal part of me knows more than my ego does, so I need to listen to that part.

Weddings

Weddings are exciting, and when they occur in a dream they often speak of a great union. Since a dream is seeking to bring us into wholeness, it always desires the integration of the various aspects of our inner life. The shadow figures, which are hidden in the darkness of our hearts, are usually brought into consciousness first and yielded to God for correction and growth. Then the masculine and feminine traits may be brought into conscious balance. This may take months or even years.

There comes a time, however, when the person begins to dream of preparing for a wedding. It is the wedding of the shadow figure with the masculine or feminine aspect. It is a sign of wholeness. That does not mean, of course, that no more growth is necessary, but it does indicate that an integration of the personality is taking place.

The "Aha!" Moment

The great questions are "How do you know if the interpretation is correct? May there not be many interpretations to the same dream? And who can tell which one is right"

These are valid questions, and fortunately there are also correct answers. It is the dreamer who will finally know the right interpretation to his or her dream. Therefore, as we help people to find the meaning of their dreams, we may make various suggestions, but we must wait for the dreamer's recognition of the one that is correct. As the dreamer thinks through his own dream with various possibilities of what it may mean, suddenly his eyes will light up and he will know. We call that the "aha!" moment.

It is the moment of recognition. Some say that though we may consider various possibilities, we must wait patiently for one to "click." We will then know which is the right interpretation. This is something we must constantly wait for as we help people with their dreams, and insist that others do the same. It is demonstrated clearly in the Scriptures.

It is possible that the magicians and wise men in Pharaoh's court made various suggestions of possible interpretations to the king's dream, yet none fit. We do know that Pharaoh was not satisfied with them. When Joseph gave his interpretation it "seemed good to Pharaoh and to all his officials. So Pharaoh asked them, 'Can we find anyone like this man, one in whom is the spirit of God.' Then Pharaoh said to Joseph, 'Since God has made all this know to you, there is no one so discerning and wise as you. You shall be in charge of my palace, and all my people are to submit to your orders' " (Gen. 41:37-40a). It is evident that through the correct interpretation of the dream, Pharaoh was persuaded of its validity and of Joseph's integrity.

The same was true for Nebuchadnezzar. Even though none of the magicians, enchanters, sorcerers, or astrologers could interpret the king's dream, and though Daniel was only a captive slave, when Daniel interpreted the dream, the king was more than impressed. He fell prostrate before Daniel and said, "Surely our God is the God of gods and the Lord of kings and a revealer of mysteries" (Dan. 2:47b). Neither Nebuchadnezzar nor Pharaoh argued about the interpretations they received. They knew without question that the interpretations were right.

For this to happen we must open ourselves up to the Holy Spirit's enlightenment. One psychiatrist did that and, as I wrote in my journal, "was so thrilled that not only she was helped, but that she was able to counsel her clients with joy and new power. This was very meaningful to the client and also to her assistant."

To prepare ourselves for ministry to others, we must learn to listen to God, as Daniel did, and observe how God spoke to his servants in time past. When we have gained a proper understanding of dreams by working on our own dreams for several years and have received help from others, we can then begin to help others too.

If we remain humble, not imposing our own ideas about the meaning of another's dreams, then we need not be afraid of a wrong interpretation. Sometimes we will not find any right interpretation and will have to wait for the answer to come. It is better to do that than to get a wrong interpretation. With such an attitude we will not feel responsible for immediately knowing the meaning of every dream. We are there to help the dreamer find the meaning, not to give an answer every time. Perhaps we may only give a suggestion so that the dreamer can wait further to find the true meaning. It is fun to see "the light go on" and the dreamer know that he or she has the right interpretation.

Chapter 19

Visions

Visions are like dreams, but they come when one is awake. Sometimes, however, it is hard to tell whether one is awake or asleep when the picture comes. Therefore, the words "dreams" and "visions" are used interchangeable in the Scriptures. Daniel, for example, spoke of the "dream and the visions" that came to Nebuchadnezzar (Dan. 2:28). Later we read, "Daniel had a dream, and visions passed through his mind as he was lying on his bed." Significantly, he "wrote down the substance of his dream" (Dan. 7:1b).

Nebuchadnezzar's first dream was revealed to Daniel in a vision (Dan. 2:19). Later Daniel told of the amazing visions that passed through his mind concerning the nations (see Dan. 7–8). He was not a monk, spending all his time in prayer; but he was ruler over the entire province of Babylon. After one of the great visions he said, "I, Daniel, was exhausted and lay ill for several days. Then I got up and went about the king's business. I was appalled by the vision; it was beyond understanding" (Dan. 8:27).

A vision is the opening of the eyes so that they can see the invisible but real spiritual world. Such was the case with Elisha's servant. The king of Aram sent horses and chariots and soldiers and surrounded the town of Dothan to capture Elisha, the prophet. In the morning Elisha's servant was afraid and cried out,

> *Oh, my lord, what shall we do? "Don't be afraid," the prophet answered. "Those who are with us are more than those who are with them." And Elisha prayed, "O Lord, open his eyes so he may see." Then the Lord opened the servant's eyes, and he looked and saw the hills full of horses and chariots of fire all around Elisha.* (2 Kings 6:15-17)

While we were in Mexico a missionary escorted us to a little town beside a mountain and told us of a visionary experience. In that town were a group of Christians greatly persecuted by the townspeople; so they built some huts up on the side of the mountain and lived there. One night while the pastor was away, because of the danger, the pastor's wife gathered the Christians together for prayer.

In the morning some of the Christians went down to the town below and were amazed that the people looked at them in awe. Never before had that happened; instead the townspeople had despised them. When the Christians inquired, they learned that the night before some of the men had gone up to burn down the huts of the Christians. To their amazement and consternation, the men had met an army. It was not a Mexican army, nor American, but the army of the Lord—angelic forces protecting the Christians. Seeing such an army by vision has been reported in both world wars and in many other wars.

Speaking of children and their guardian angels, Jesus said, "See that you do not look down on one of these little ones. For I tell you that their angels in heaven always see the face of My Father in heaven" (Mt. 18:10).

A mother told of an encouraging vision of an angel guarding her little child. The mother was concerned because their house was so near the street. She told me:

About five-thirty in the morning, as I was getting my housecoat out of the closet, I turned around and looked into my daughter's room across the hall. I stood there stunned. My husband asked me what was wrong. I told him to look into her room. He did, but he couldn't see anything except her crib. I saw a form in my child's bed. It was a little person like my child, except the hair was gold and the head was bowed, looking down at my child.

I walked over to her bedroom door to make sure I was really seeing this. As I stood there the head bowed a little more, and I knew it was an angel watching over my child. There was a beautiful presence in the room. I knew that God was telling me He had heard my prayer and that He loves us so much that He has an angel for each person in the world to watch over us. As I looked again at my child's crib, I could no longer see the angel, but I knew that God had His hand on my little child and that I could trust Him completely. I shared this vision with my child who is now three years old. Her eyes beamed when I told her about the angel.

Dr. V. Raymond Edman, the former president of Wheaton College, Wheaton, Illinois, told of this kind of an experience. Mr. and Mrs. Edman were working in Ecuador, South America, as a pair of young missionaries. Mr. Edman was quite discouraged because they did not see any results in the lives of the Quichua Indians with whom they were working. One day a Quichua woman came to their door, dressed in the typical long dress that reached almost to the ground, and wearing a man's felt hat on her head.

Young Edman opened the door to their little house, and she spoke to him at the door, greatly encouraging him about their work. He was thrilled and turned to his wife to tell her about the woman. She said, "Why did you not invite her in?" He opened the door again, but saw no one. This was more than surprising; it seemed impossible.

The fields bordering the roads and villages of Ecuador have six-foot mud walls instead of fences to keep the grazing animals in, for mud is cheaper than wire. From one little house to the next along the way there are often continuous walls. The house next to the Edman's was a long way off, with only a straight wall joining them, and only a continuous wall on the other side of the house, and a wall on the other side of the road. Yet immediately after the Quichua woman had left, he looked out and could see no one on that little road. The woman could not have arrived at the next house in that minute or less. As the Edmans examined the situation and considered the message given by the woman, they concluded that she must have been an angel revealed by vision. In Scripture, angels often came dressed for the occasion so that the people would not be frightened by them.

These encouraging visionary experiences may come only occasionally to individual people, but they are not uncommon in general. There may also be a call from the Lord through a vision, as with Samuel (see 1 Sam. 3).

144

When I was teaching African pastors in Zaire, the seminary president said that many of their students had received their call to the pastoral ministry through visions. This was a little difficult for an American to receive.

A vision and a dream are basically the same, but there is one difference in the handling of certain visions. When a person is praying for another and receives a vision, the final interpretation of that vision belongs to the one for whom it is given. When such a vision is received it is usually good to tell the person for whom you are praying what the vision was, but then ask, "Does that mean anything to you?" Usually it will be understood by the person for whom it is given, and will be very meaningful. There was one occasion where the meaning of a vision was suggested to me, but I knew it was not right.

During a twenty-two month period when we had no home, we stored our furniture and belongings and traveled about teaching. We longed for a home, and as we drove around the beautiful area where we were speaking, we would see a house with a nice setting, and say, "Doesn't that look inviting? Wouldn't that be a nice place for a home?" At that time Lillie and I were teaching a small group in a Mennonite church in Ontario. The subject was the voice of God. That evening I was speaking on learning to listen to that voice.

During the day my pastor in Michigan called to say that he believed that he had found just the house for us, inasmusch as we had to have a certain kind of arrangement since we were away from home so much. The pastor said it was urgent, and he even offered to have someone fly us in on a little plane if we would return to look at the house. We had been looking for so long that we were doubtful that this was the house, but appreciated the offer. So we suggested to the little group that they listen to the Lord with us to see if we might get directions about going to see the house.

I think it is important to pay careful attention to what we hear when we ask for prayer, and record the words that we receive from others. That evening about ten different people received the same kind of direction saying that we were not to go. One man, however, said his wife had had a vision, which was quite unusual in those early days, but she thought it might help us determine where we ought to live, for we did not even know in which country we should live.

This woman saw a vision of a huge, green maple tree. It was so large that it filled her vision. She tried to look around the tree, and finally succeeded, and she saw the Lord behind the tree.

Since the maple leaf is the national emblem of Canada, she suggested that the vision meant that we should live in that country.

I knew immediately that this interpretation was not correct. I said, "No, that is not what it means. Rather it means that Canada has so filled our vision that we cannot see the Lord any more." The woman was praying for us, so the vision belonged to us, and we had the final right of interpretation. This is an important principle, for sometimes people project onto others what they think is the meaning of the vision instead of letting the one for whom it has been given interpret it.

Many of the prophets' messages came out of visions. How beautiful is the vision of our Lord Jesus Christ that John gives, with the whole future of the Church and the final revelation of Heaven. Without visions we would see only the material world.

Visions may be seen in different ways. One may see them as if they were a movie on television. Another may see them in imagination, while meditating upon God's Word. Others find it very difficult to see a vision, because they think they should see it the same as others.

God wants us to see as Jesus did when He told the disciples to find the room to prepare for the Passover meal.

So He sent two of His disciples, telling them, "Go into the city, and a man carrying a jar of water will meet you. Follow him. Say to the owner of the house he enters, 'The Teacher asks: Where is My guest room, where I may eat the Passover with My disciples?' He will show you a large upper room, furnished and ready. Make preparations for us there." The disciples left, went into the city and found things just as Jesus had told them. (Mk. 14:13-16a)

Evidently Jesus had seen that scene in a vision and believed it and acted upon it.

God uses the faculties of the mind, the imagination, intuition, and probably much more to help us understand what He is saying and assist us in the work we are to do. We have exercised so few gifts, but are constantly amazed as He reveals more and more to us. Let us do what the prophet Habakkuk says, "I will stand at my watch and station myself on the ramparts; I will look to see what He will say to me" (Hab. 2:1a). Let us also look to see what He will say to us.

147

Chapter 20

Lessons from Dreams of National Importance

Throughout the Bible we find many dreams of national significance. The dreams of Abraham, Pharaoh, and Daniel are examples of such dreams and demonstrate the need for reliable interpreters.

Abram's dream assured him of the founding of the nation of Israel:

As the sun was setting, Abram fell into a deep sleep, and a thick and dreadful darkness came over him. Then the Lord said to him, "Know for certain that your descendants will be strangers in a country not their own, and they will be enslaved and mistreated four hundred years. But I will punish the nation they serve as slaves, and afterward they

*will come out with great possessions...To your decendants
I give this land, from the river of Egypt to the great river,
the Euphrates.* (Genesis 15:12-14,18b)

This dream was quite literal and direct and needed no
further interpretation. Then God continued the history of
Israel with a dream reported by the king of Egypt.

*In my dream I was standing on the bank of the Nile, when
out of the river there came up seven cows, fat and sleek,
and they grazed among the reeds. After them, seven other
cows came up—scrawny and very ugly and lean. I had
never seen such ugly cows in all the land of Egypt. The
lean, ugly cows ate up the seven fat cows that came up
first. But even after they ate them, no one could tell that
they had done so; they looked just as ugly as before. Then
I woke up. In my dream I also saw seven head of grain,
full and good, growing on a single stalk. After them, seven
other heads sprouted—withered and thin and scorched by
the east wind. The thin heads of grain swallowed up the
seven good heads.* (Genesis 41:17-24a)

The dream of Pharaoh was quite different from the
one given to Abram. This was a symbolic dream, and none
of the Egyptian interpreters of dreams could explain it to
him. Joseph, however, had the Spirit of God in him, and
he gave us some good principles of interpretation. He said
first that the two dreams were one. This is a pattern, for
usually when we have two or three dreams in succession in
one night, they are all saying the same thing in different
ways. It is as if we are trying to explain a matter to a friend,
but he does not understand, so we change to a different
picture and try to say the same thing in a new way.

In Pharaoh's dream the symbols of the cows and heads of grain were used to say the same thing. Numbers are important in dreams. In this case the number seven referred to seven years. In the butler's and baker's dreams, the number three referred to days. In these instances the numbers were used symbolically to refer to years or days. The numbers one, three, four, six, seven, twelve, forty, one hundred, and one thousand are used symbolically in the Bible; therefore we must be very careful that we don't always take numbers literally.

The dream was clear and needed to be acted upon. Pharaoh knew that the interpretation was correct, for it is the dreamer who will finally recognize the right interpretation of his or her dream. This dream of Pharaoh saved Egypt, but in God's plan it also saved Israel.

Next we turn to the Book of Daniel for the great dreams of Nebuchadnezzar, the king of Babylon. Daniel may well have seen his parents killed as he was taken captive and carried away with the Babylonian army. Later he and his friends were chosen to learn the language and literature of the Babylonians because of their intellectual aptitude. All this time, they kept their hearts right before God. "To these four young men God gave knowledge and understanding of all kinds of literature and learning. And Daniel could understand visions and dreams of all kinds" (Dan. 1:17).

People sometimes say that they will not learn anything about dreams except to ask God what they mean. That is like the young prospective doctor who says he will not go to medical school because unbelievers may be teaching there. He will ask God how to take out an appendix and do by-pass surgery. That is folly! The culture of Babylon was literally filled with idolatry and all that goes with it.

We know that the prospective doctor must learn and acquire knowledge, and then ask God for wisdom concerning how to use it. In the same way there is a vast amount of knowledge that we need to learn and discern about dreams from whatever sources it may be found. Then we can ask for wisdom in the use of such knowledge.

Daniel had prepared himself and then the challenge came. The king had a nightmare, so frightening and troubling that he could not sleep; however, afterward he could not remember the dream. This is not strange. A dream may often leave a deep impression on the mind, even though we cannot remember its content. Though the king was determined to know the dream and its meaning, the astrologers said it was impossible. That was where Daniel and his friends were willing to risk their lives.

They began to pray for an answer so that God might save their lives. God heard their prayer and gave them a vision of what the king had dreamed. Then they praised the God of Heaven and went to the executioner and asked to see the king, again at the risk of their lives. But they also asked to save the lives of the astrologers. As Daniel and his friends were brought to the king, Daniel said that answering the king's request was impossible for man, but not for God. We need to learn all we can, but then ask God for help, for He can give the gift of wisdom and knowledge.

Daniel even told Nebuchadnezzar the setting of the dream. As the king had been lying on his bed thinking about the future, God had intervened. Often dreams come as an answer to what we have been seeking in other ways. Then Daniel went on to say that the answer came to him not because of his greater wisdom (in other words, anyone can learn to interpret dreams) the answer came for the king's sake, so that he might know the thoughts of his heart, over against the thoughts of his mind.

"I looked," said Nebuchadnezzar. That is an accurate description of how we see the unfolding of a dream. Our eyes are actually watching a picture. A sleeper, during a dream, follows the picture that he sees.[1] This is called rapid eye movement (REM) and is one of the signs that a person is dreaming.

Daniel described what the king had seen as visions and dreams. The two words are sometime used interchangeable, for they both come from the same source. The vision breaks through our thoughts while we are awake; the dream speaks while we are asleep.

The impressiveness of the dream comes with the words "there before you stood a large statue—an enormous, dazzling statue, awesome in appearance" (Dan. 2:31b). Sometimes dreams are so vivid that they leave an unforgettable impression. We can see why the king dreamed of a statue. When our presidents retire they write their memoirs; in those days kings built statues by which to be remembered. The statue represented his kingdom and those who were to follow.

The metals of the statue decreased in value as they were described. Nebuchadnezzar was represented by the head of gold. The chest and shoulders of silver represented the next kingdom, its value being less. The statue's belly and thighs were of bronze, representing the third kingdom. "Its legs [were] of iron, its feet partly of iron and partly of baked clay" (Dan. 2:33). Then Daniel gave an interesting interpretation of the last symbol.

> *Finally, there will be a fourth kingdom, strong as iron–for iron breaks and smashes everything–and as iron breaks things to pieces, so it will crush and break all the others. Just as you saw that the feet and toes were partly of baked clay and partly or iron, so this will be a divided kingdom; yet it will have some of the strength of iron in it, even as you saw iron mixed with clay. As the toes were partly iron and partly clay, so this kingdom will be partly strong and partly brittle. And just as you saw the iron mixed with baked clay, so the people will be a mixture and will not remain united, any more than iron mixes with clay.* (Daniel 2:40-43)

Dreams often show the present situation and then what will happen if we continue to go the way we are going. In this case, it first described the natural pattern and then showed God's intervention. "While you were watching, a rock was cut out, but not by human hands" (Dan. 2:34a). Relative to the gold, silver, bronze, and iron, the rock was of little value. And so would that Kingdom be appraised by the world.

If we look ahead we know that the rock represented Jesus Christ coming in His humanity, despised by mankind. Now comes a detail that is of great significance. The rock cut out of the mountain without human work signified the virgin birth of Jesus. He did not come by man's intervention. The details of a dream are often of great significance and must not be ignored.

The rock struck the statue on its feet of iron and clay, thus beginning with the last kingdom and working its way back to the first, destroying them all, prefiguring Christ's Kingdom. The wind blew all the other kingdoms away like dust. Then the rock became a mountain and filled the whole earth. In this dream Nebuchadnezzar was told that though his kingdom was the most valuable, it would be wiped away by the Kingdom to come. Daniel was confident of his interpretation: "The dream is true and the interpretation is trustworthy" (Dan. 2:45b).

Then an amazing thing happened. The mighty monarch of Babylon fell before his captive slave, Daniel, and honored him. He ordered that an offering and incense be presented to him as though he were a god. The king said, "Surely your God is the God of gods and the Lord of kings and a revealer of mysteries, for you were able to reveal this mystery" (Dan. 2:47b). We see in this dream another wonderful example of symbolic language. It is a foretelling of the story of the nations.

King Nebuchadnezzar believed in Daniel's God, but did he believe in God for himself? As a counselor, hearing his declaration we might have thought so, but the dream shows his heart rather than just his words. Did he believe in God? Quite the contrary. In the next scene, instead of remembering that the statue in the dream would be destroyed, he built a huge statue of himself, ninety feet high and nine feet wide, and ordered that everyone bow down to it.

He was challenged by Daniel's friends, however, who as faithful Jews refused to bow down to the statue. The king was furious and ordered that they be thrown into a blazing furnace. He said, "Then what god will be able to rescue you from my hand?" (Dan. 3:15b). He had not yet bowed to the God of Heaven, so God sent him another dream, the kind of repeated dreams God sends when people do not listen the first time.

The king told the dream to Daniel. First he described the setting of the dream. "I, Nebuchadnezzar, was at home in my palace, contented and prosperous. I had a dream that made me afraid. As I was lying in my bed, the images and visions that passed through my mind terrified me (Dan. 4:4-5). Again he found no one to interpret his frightening dream, but he remembered Daniel. This so often happens: people forget all about their source of help until they come into a time of desperate need. Once again the dream showed him first his present situation.

> *I looked, and there before me stood a tree in the middle of the land. Its height was enormous. The tree grew large and strong and its top touched the sky; it was visible to the ends of the earth. Its leaves were beautiful, its fruit abundant, and on it was food for all. Under it the beasts of the field found shelter, and the birds of the air lived in its branches; from it every creature was fed.* (Daniel 4:10b-12)

This time the king was represented by a tree. The statue spoke of that which was finished; he was thinking of his death. The tree spoke of life and growth for him personally. He was contented and prosperous. His was a great nation, and all the world paid attention to it. Its government was caring for the needs of all the peoples. Then came the part of the dream that told what would happen if he continued to go in the direction he was going.

> *In the visions I saw while lying in my bed, I looked, and there before me was a messenger, a holy one, coming down from heaven. He called in a loud voice: "Cut down the*

tree and trim off its branches; strip off its leaves and scatter its fruit. Let the animals flee from under it and the birds from its branches. But let the stump and its roots, bound with iron and bronze, remain in the ground, in the grass of the field." (Daniel 4:13-15a)

Now the supernatural entered in, as in the first dream with the rock cut out of the mountain without hands. This was frightening, for it was beyond the king's control. The voice was important in the dream, and this was a loud voice. The statue in the earlier dream, which was man-made, spoke of his kingdom; the tree spoke of him personally. He was to be cut off from his throne, and the kingdom would be affected by it.

Now came another detail: "Let the stump and its roots, bound with iron and bronze, remain in the ground, in the grass of the field." This was going to prove important, for like a tree in a tropical country, it could grow again. In the meantime he would be bound, not in a prison or an asylum, but in the grass of the field.

Let him be drenched with the dew of heaven, and let him live with the animals among the plants of the earth. Let his mind be changed from that of a man and let him be given the mind of an animal, till seven times pass by for him. (Daniel 4:15-16)

Now we see one of the peculiarities of the dream, for the tree changed into a man. Literally this is impossible, but symbolically it continued the story, for the dream now became very personal. The picture was taken from the way the mentally insane were dealt with in those days. Instead of being put in hospitals as is done today, these people were left free to roam like animals. That is what the dream

157

said would happen. Even with the warning there was mercy, for he would be given seven years in his insanity to repent. He was even told that the messenger, or angel, had given the dream for a purpose.

The decision is announced by messengers, the holy ones declare the verdict, so that the living may know that the Most High is sovereign over the kingdoms of men and gives them to anyone he wishes and sets over them the lowliest of men. (Daniel 4:17)

God had given the king a warning, and it was up to him to respond to it. Apparently it moved him enough so that he paid attention for a year, but then he lifted his heart in pride and said, "Is not this the great Babylon I have built as the royal residence, by my mighty power and for the glory of my majesty?" Then, suddenly, while "the words were still on his lips," a voice from Heaven said that exactly what he had been warned about was now going to happen. Nebuchadnezzar lost his mind and for seven years he was like an animal. Finally he repented and said, "At the end of that time, I, Nebuchadnezzar, raised my eyes toward heaven, and my sanity was restored. Then I praised the Most High; I honored and glorified Him who lives forever" (Dan. 4:34).

He was restored to his throne, and his honor and splendor returned to him. "Now, I Nebuchadnezzar, praise and exalt and glorify the King of heaven, because everything he does is right and all his ways are just" (Dan. 4:37a). The dream had done its work. The mighty king of Babylon was humbled and God was exalted. This was the final purpose of the dream.

After Nebuchadnezzar had died, his son, Belshazzar, forgot the lesson his father had learned. Again God gave

His warning, not simply by word, but by graphic illustration. As Belshazzar the king ordered that the sacred vessels which were taken from the temple in Jerusalem be brought in, he and his nobles and wives drank from them, and "praised the gods of gold and silver, of bronze, iron, wood and stone" (Dan. 5:4b).

Suddenly the fingers of a human hand appeared and wrote on the plaster wall near the lampstand in the royal palace. The king watched the hand as it wrote. His face turned pale, and he was so frightened that his knees knocked together and his legs gave way. (Daniel 5:5-6)

Daniel was called upon to interpret the message, which said, "Your kingdom is divided and given to the Medes and Persians" (Dan. 5:29). That night the kingdom of Babylon fell.

The greatest test of the dream interpreter came as Daniel distinguished himself with the next great empire, the Medes and Persians. In this situation, he was willing to face the possibility of being thrown into the lions' den for his faith, but God sent his angel to protect Daniel. It is not a light thing to be an interpreter of dreams.

From there on Daniel had great visions and dreams of the nations. On one occasion he was wrestling in prayer in behalf of his own nation, Israel, when he saw an awesome vision and described it:

I looked up and there before me was a man dressed in linen, with a belt of the finest gold around His waist. His body was like chrysolite, His face like lightning, His eyes like flaming torches, His arms and legs like the gleam of burnished bronze, and His voice like the sound of a multitude (Dan. 10:5-6).

The vision left Daniel terror-stricken. The spiritual battle was on. The angel of the Lord had sought to reach Daniel and said:

> *But the prince of the Persian kingdom resisted me twenty-one days. Then Michael, one of the chief princes, came to help me, because I was detained there with the King of Persia....Soon I will return to fight against the Prince of Persia, and when I go, the prince of Greece will come.* (Daniel 10:13,20b)

God is still speaking to kings, presidents, and prime ministers, but few Daniels are there to interpret for them what God is saying. It is not a light matter to become an interpreter of dreams to those in high authority. The time may well be at hand when God is calling some to that task.

Chapter 21

Important Principles of Dream Interpretation

Above all the knowledge that they may gain, the interpreters of dreams must be open and honest, willing to see what God wants to show them. The first beatitude is to become their attitude. "Blessed are the poor in spirit, for theirs is the kingdom of heaven" (Mt. 5:3). Those who recognize their poverty of spirit will always be willing to learn, whereas those who say, "I am rich; I have acquired wealth and do not need a thing,...do not realize that [they] are wretched, pitiful, poor, blind and naked" (Rev. 3:17). They will not be open to see what God wants to show them.

God has so much to reveal to his people, and His wisdom is so far beyond understanding. He says, "As the heavens are higher than the earth, so are My ways higher than your ways and My thoughts than your thoughts" (Is. 55:9). The purpose of dreams and visions is to break through our rational thought patterns to show us what we have not heard or believed before. It therefore takes great humility to understand what God is saying in this symbolic language, more humility than knowledge.

We must pay attention to our dreams and visions as though it is God Himself speaking to us. It is important that we write down the essence of our dreams immediately, having a pen and pad handy to scribble down the details, which tend to vanish away once the mind becomes active. Furthermore, we must write down the whole dream before we begin trying to interpret it, or much of it will be lost.

Once we recognize that dreams are a way by which God speaks to us, we will be willing to discipline ourselves to catch all that He shows us. A journal of our spiritual life, which will contain our dreams and their interpretations, will become a great treasure. It will become a guide by which we can check our inmost thoughts.

There must also be a willingness to obey what God is saying to us in our dreams and visions. If we will not obey the dreams, we will not long be able to understand them. Of course, God is very patient, and He may repeat dreams and even nightmares to awaken us. But if we fail to listen to Him, He may allow us to be overcome by worse conditions (see Job 33:13-22).

We must always remember that the mind speaks in the language of reason and concepts, but dreams speak in the language of riddles and parables. The language of pictures and symbols is universal and powerful, but it is the language of a child. Jesus said, "Unless you change and become like little children, you will never enter the kingdom of heaven" (Mt. 18:3b).

This morning I was concerned about a couple for whom we were praying. Very succinctly God showed me what potential problem I needed to avoid.

I dreamed I was watching a baseball game, but I was standing near the batter where a foul ball might hit me, and I heard a loud voice, "Get off the playing field!"

Though I certainly needed to continue praying, I saw clearly that I was not a player in the game, so I was to get out of the way or I might get hurt by a "foul" ball. By this picture God revealed an important truth.

We must be careful not to take symbolic pictures literally. How foolish it would be to interpret my dream that I am literally to get off a baseball field, for I have nothing to do with baseball. The symbolic language must be constantly applied, which is often hard for us to do, since we in the western world have been trained to think so rationally. Always keep in mind that dreams speak symbolically, except in a few cases where God will make it clear to our hearts that He is speaking literally.

Our initial approach to interpreting a dream ought to be that we know nothing about it. We must be open to anything it has to say. Then we will be ready for any possible insight that the dream may give. We listen to the heart for the meaning, not trying to reason it out with the mind. We wait for possible associations to the symbols. We remember the setting in which the dream has come. What is it saying?

One of the reasons we have a hard time understanding our own dreams is because they show us those aspects of ourselves that we try to keep hidden. Others, especially our husbands or wives, will see those aspects of our personality better than we; therefore, it is good to work with someone we trust to help us with our dreams.

Remember that most of the time dreams speak subjectively, that is, about ourselves, even when we dream about other people. Just as the Bible has much more to say about what we are to do than what we are to tell others that they are to do, so our dreams speak mostly about ourselves. I find it true overall that about ninety-five percent of all dreams are subjective and only about five percent are objective. In Chapter 10 I have explained what to do about objective dreams.

It is especially important when helping others that we do not insist on our own interpretation of a symbol or of the dream itself. We must remember that ultimately it is the dreamer alone who will be able to recognize the right interpretation of his or her dream. The dream uses symbols familiar to the dreamer, and the dreamer will recognize their meanings.

Remember that the dream may have many levels of understanding. Just as with the Scriptures, we may at first only understand the meaning at surface level and only gradually understand more and more. Dreams, however, do not have opposite meanings. If one interprets a dream in one way and another just the opposite, then we know that there is something wrong.

If a dream seems to be saying something contradictory to what the Scriptures say, this should immediately raise a serious question. It is possible that it may be saying the opposite of what our traditional interpretation of the Bible has been, yet is not speaking against the basic doctrines, such as the Ten Commandments. God does not contradict Himself.

Dreams speak to believers and unbelievers alike, and are designed to eventually lead each person into a living relationship with God. Therefore, do not try to run ahead of the dream when helping others. Remember that God knows exactly where the dreamer is spiritually and what language He may use with them. When Saddam Hussein dreamed that Mohammed told him that his guns were pointing the wrong way, we needed not be alarmed. God knew that at that time Saddam would listen to Mohammed rather than Jesus, so He framed the message accordingly.

There is no better counselor than a dream through which God speaks to us by His Spirit. It is like a mirror, and since it is God's mirror, it is always accurate. Though always accurate, it may not always be complimentary. But its purpose is to show us what our condition is. Though dreams reveal in most vivid ways, they never condemn.

Like a mirror, a dream may have the most value when it reflects what is wrong with us. Therefore, we do not become the judge of the dream but let the dream judge us. The danger of deciding that some dreams are valid and others are not is that then we make ourselves the judge of the dream. Therefore, we will most likely choose the dreams that we like and discard the rest.

God is eager to speak to His people whom He has created. To do so He has a pattern of communication. God speaks, then He reveals. We need to recognize the relationship between the voice of God and dreams, for dreams are not the direct voice of God but the indirect voice. By dreams and visions He explains and illustrates His point. He is so gracious and patient that He finds unique ways to get His message across to us. Therefore, we need to learn to listen and understand what He is saying.

Your dream is a message from God specifically for you. Never force your interpretation upon another's dream. And never accept an interpretation of your dream with which your heart is not at peace.

Receive your dream and let it gently speak to your heart; it will lead you to wholeness and to all the potential that God sees in you. God has much more in mind for you than you can imagine, and He is willing to show you through dreams and visions, just as He does through Scripture. What greater privilege than to be able to receive vivid messages and illustrations of communication from the living God, and to act upon them!

Inspirational and Study Books by Herman Riffel

Dream Interpretation, a Biblical Understanding. Destiny Image—"Your book reveals deep study, sound scholarship, great helpfulness. It will help many get a biblical view of dreams, one which will prove helpful in personal growth" (Francis Whiting, D. Min., D.D.).

Dreams: Giants and Geniuses in the Making. Destiny Image—This book tells of scientists, statesmen, inventors and composers of music as well as religious leaders who have received their inspiration and direction through dreams, and gives basic principles of dream interpretation.

Christian Dream Interpretation

Seminars

Herman and Lillie Riffel offer dream seminars on the Christian perspective of dream interpretation. They have had 25 years of experience in dream interpretation and 50 years of spiritual ministry in lecture tours that have taken them through nearly 50 countries.

Dream Therapy Workshops

Small local workshops are conducted in a series of six two-hour sessions. Deep work of the heart is done by the Holy Spirit as God reveals problems, promises, and guidance through the dreams of those participating.

Order Form

Books

( ) *Dream Interpretation, a Biblical Understanding* $10.95
( ) *Dream: Giants and Geniuses in the Making* . . . . $ 8.95

Video and Audio Tape Series

Christian Dream Interpretation

( ) 22 half-hour video-taped lectures $65.00
( ) 11 hours of audio-taped lectures. $49.00
( ) Study manual. . . . . $ 6.95

Spiritual Principles Involved in Psychological Counseling

( ) 12 half-hour video-taped lectures $45.00
( ) 6 hours of audio-taped lectures. $29.95
( ) Study manual. . . . . $ 4.95

Christian Maturity and the Spirit's Power

( ) 8 hours of audio-taped lectures. $35.00

U.S. Postage and Handling (per item): Books $2.00; Tape Albums $3.00
Order total, including postage $ _____

Direct all orders and inquiries to:
Herman H. Riffel
2404 Dominion Dr. 1B
Frederick, MD 21702
Tel: 301-668-9518; email: riffelh@crosslink.net

Name _____

Address _____

City, State, Zip _____

Prices valid through 2001